TExES

English Language Arts and Reading 4-8 Practice Questions

TExES Practice Tests & Exam Review for the Texas Examinations of Educator Standards

Mometrix

TEST PREPARATION

Dear Future Exam Success Story

First of all, **THANK YOU** for purchasing Mometrix study materials!

Second, congratulations! You are one of the few determined test-takers who are committed to doing whatever it takes to excel on your exam. **You have come to the right place.** We developed these practice tests with one goal in mind: to deliver you the best possible approximation of the questions you will see on test day.

Standardized testing is one of the biggest obstacles on your road to success, which only increases the importance of doing well in the high-pressure, high-stakes environment of test day. Your results on this test could have a significant impact on your future, and these practice tests will give you the repetitions you need to build your familiarity and confidence with the test content and format to help you achieve your full potential on test day.

Your success is our success

We would love to hear from you! If you would like to share the story of your exam success or if you have any questions or comments in regard to our products, please contact us at **800-673-8175** or **support@mometrix.com**.

Thanks again for your business and we wish you continued success!

Sincerely,
The Mometrix Test Preparation Team

Copyright © 2026 by Mometrix Media LLC. All rights reserved.
Printed in the United States of America

TABLE OF CONTENTS

Practice Test #1

Foundations of Reading

1. Which of the following options is an example of a formal reading assessment?

a. Student interviews
b. Guided reading observations
c. State reading test
d. Anecdotal records

2. What is a primary purpose for giving an Informal Reading Inventory to a student?

a. To track the texts and genres a student has read over the course of the school year
b. To help students identify books of personal interest
c. To determine which reading behaviors students have developed prior to entering formal schooling
d. To match students with appropriate instructional texts

3. Of the following, which is most correct in regard to children matching voice to print?

a. It is not normal for a second grader to finger-point to words when reading.
b. Giving young children creative, fun pointers is wrong, as these are crutches.
c. Older student finger-pointing shows reading struggles and impedes fluency.
d. Using bookmarks/popsicle sticks sideways has no effect on finger-pointing.

4. Which of the following is LEAST accurate about ongoing informal assessments for English language Learners (ELLs)?

a. Ongoing informal assessments are able to demonstrate ELLs' content knowledge more validly than formal tests.
b. Ongoing informal assessments are usually more motivating for ELLs than formal tests.
c. Ongoing informal assessments are usually harder for ELLs to complete than formal tests.
d. Ongoing informal assessments provide the teacher with opportunity for more individualized instruction.

5. Cognates and realia are most useful for teaching which component of reading instruction to ELLs?

a. Vocabulary
b. Prosody
c. Phonological awareness
d. Phonemic awareness

6. *Train, brain, spring.* The underlined letters are examples of:

a. Consonant digraph
b. Consonant blend
c. Consonant shift
d. Continental shift

Copyright © Mometrix Media. You have been licensed one copy of this document for personal use only. Any other reproduction or redistribution is strictly prohibited. All rights reserved.
This content is provided for test preparation purposes only and does not imply an endorsement by Mometrix of any particular political, scientific, or religious point of view.

7. VC, CVC, CCVC, CVCC, and CCVCC are among the types of:

a. Homophones
b. Closed syllables
c. Monosyllabic words
d. Polyglotal indicators

8. What is one benefit of implicit phonics instruction?

a. It leads to stronger decoding skills.
b. Its progression from part to whole increases proficiency more quickly.
c. Research suggests it is the most effective approach to phonics instruction.
d. Phonics skills are taught in a meaningful context.

9. Which of the following words consists of one free morpheme and one affix?

a. Unhelpful
b. Previewing
c. Truck
d. Friendless

10. Research has indicated that which of the following options is the best predictor of early reading success?

a. Phonemic awareness
b. Interest in reading
c. Concepts of print
d. Oral vocabulary

11. Which choice represents a likely progression of phonological awareness skills?

a. Onset and rime manipulation, rhyming, phoneme deletion, syllabification
b. Phoneme deletion, syllabification, onset and rime manipulation, rhyming
c. Rhyming, syllabification, onset and rime manipulation, phoneme deletion
d. Syllabification, phoneme deletion, rhyming, onset and rime manipulation

12. On a continuum, which of these represents the most complex level of phonological awareness?

a. Segmenting words into their individual syllables and blending individual syllables into words
b. Phonemic awareness, i.e., understanding words consist of phonemes and manipulating these
c. Segmenting words into their onsets and rimes and blending onsets and rimes into full words
d. Segmenting sentences, i.e., understanding speech consists of separate words, and rhyming songs

13. Which of the following words contains an r-controlled vowel?

a. Rock
b. Short
c. Rain
d. Trace

Copyright © Mometrix Media. You have been licensed one copy of this document for personal use only. Any other reproduction or redistribution is strictly prohibited. All rights reserved.
This content is provided for test preparation purposes only and does not imply an endorsement by Mometrix of any particular political, scientific, or religious point of view.

14. A sentence in a book states, "The furry dog chases the stick." Which of the following examples demonstrates a structural error, if stated by a student reading the text?

a. The furry dog chases the branch.
b. The furry dog chases the big stick.
c. The fuzzy dog chases the stick.
d. The furry dog chased the stick.

15. Of the following influences on student reading comprehension, which one is a psychological factor?

a. Attention
b. Perception
c. Motivation
d. Working memory

16. The words *classify*, *measure*, and *observe* are examples of what?

a. Listening vocabulary
b. Academic vocabulary
c. Receptive vocabulary
d. Expressive vocabulary

17. Among these effective instructional strategies for building and extending vocabulary knowledge, which one is implicit?

a. Context skills
b. Root analysis
c. Word maps
d. Keywords

18. A student is reading a fictional book and reaches the following sentence: "Unlike Mark, whose college plans were tentative, Ana already had firm plans to attend the state university." Which type of context clue is present in this sentence to help the student determine the meaning of *tentative*?

a. Synonym clue
b. Definition clue
c. Antonym clue
d. Inference clue

19. Which of the following options best demonstrates a kinesthetic activity to build sight word recognition?

a. Circling sight words found in a magazine article
b. Building sight words with letter tiles
c. Reading books containing numerous sight words
d. Hopping along sight words written in chalk

Copyright © Mometrix Media. You have been licensed one copy of this document for personal use only. Any other reproduction or redistribution is strictly prohibited. All rights reserved.
This content is provided for test preparation purposes only and does not imply an endorsement by Mometrix of any particular political, scientific, or religious point of view.

20. Prior to launching a sixth-grade genre study on historical fiction, Mrs. Perez plans to create a list of vocabulary words to explicitly teach to her students. She wants to select tier-two words that will best contribute to students' overall language development and allow them to transfer their knowledge to other reading experiences. Which words fit these criteria?

a. Challenging but common vocabulary words that carry a lot of meaning
b. High-frequency, concrete nouns
c. Domain-specific words found in students' social studies textbooks
d. Student-selected words related to their interests within the genre

21. Which of these best describes the "during reading" phase of whole-class reading instruction with a focus on decoding phonological patterns?

a. Partners reading a text together and help one another decode new words as they encounter them.
b. Teachers monitor student progress and provide assistance when necessary while independently reading through an assigned text.
c. Students read the text as partners and take turns reading and listening to one another.
d. Teachers read sentences aloud, demonstrating decoding practices. Students then repeat together as a class.

22. Which of these applies the principle of teaching from simpler to more complex for instruction in decoding multisyllabic words?

a. Teaching open syllables first among syllable pattern types
b. Teaching closed syllables first among syllable pattern types
c. Teaching syllabication before introducing multisyllabic words
d. Teaching syllable patterns based upon spelling generalizations

23. Some teachers have integrated smartphones into school curriculum as a way of using available technology to support the learning and practice of student research. What is correct about this trend?

a. Smartphones are projected to become too expensive as teaching tools.
b. Teachers should allow students to use the resources that they have.
c. It is unnecessary for a school to create an acceptable use policy for this.
d. Teachers need to know how to get information from students' phones.

24. Researchers have found which of these about instruction in phonological awareness?

a. All children benefit highly from receiving instruction in phonological awareness.
b. Children at risk for speech or language delays benefit the most from this teaching.
c. Some children benefit little from this instruction, and some do not benefit at all.
d. This instruction only benefits children who have normal language development.

25. Which type of blending of phonemes into words is the best technique for diagnostically pinpointing individual student problem areas in phonics instruction?

a. Successive blending
b. Silent blending
c. Final blending
d. Line blending

Copyright © Mometrix Media. You have been licensed one copy of this document for personal use only. Any other reproduction or redistribution is strictly prohibited. All rights reserved.
This content is provided for test preparation purposes only and does not imply an endorsement by Mometrix of any particular political, scientific, or religious point of view.

26. In which stage of spelling development do children typically learn the alphabetic principle?

a. In Stage 1
b. In Stage 3
c. In Stage 2
d. In Stage 4

27. What description best represents how teachers promote language, literacy, and reading development by integrating it into their classroom instruction?

a. The teacher asks students during a science lesson to state hypotheses, observations, and conclusions orally.
b. The teacher asks students during a science lesson to write down hypotheses, observations, and conclusions.
c. The teacher models language and literacy participation by demonstrating writing apart from class discussion.
d. The teacher provides games that require students read, write, and act out target content in small groups.

Refer to the following for question 28:

As part of a new literacy unit, a kindergarten teacher displays the following chart on the class word wall:

-all Family	
Ball	Hall
Call	Fall
Small	Wall
All	Tall

28. Which of the following additional instructional strategies could the teacher implement to reinforce the concepts introduced by the displayed chart and further develop students' reading fluency skills?

a. Including the words displayed on the chart into a weekly spelling list
b. Implementing a word-building activity using magnetic tiles based on the chart
c. Leading a choral reading activity in which the class reads aloud together from the chart
d. Having students practice tracing each word on dotted-line paper before writing them independently

29. While reading a fictional text, a fifth-grade student encounters the word *aesthetic* and asks for clarification. Which of the following responses by the teacher would most effectively prompt the student to use context clues for deciphering the meaning of the word?

a. "Look at the illustrations. Do you see any clues that might tell you what the word means?"
b. "Does the word have any prefixes or suffixes that could tell us the meaning?"
c. "Can you make an educated guess about what the word means?"
d. "Have you seen any words similar to this one before?"

Copyright © Mometrix Media. You have been licensed one copy of this document for personal use only. Any other reproduction or redistribution is strictly prohibited. All rights reserved.
This content is provided for test preparation purposes only and does not imply an endorsement by Mometrix of any particular political, scientific, or religious point of view.

Text Comprehension and Analysis

30. A fourth-grade teacher is preparing her students for a reading test in which a number of words have been replaced with blanks. The test will be multiple-choice; there are three possible answers given for each blank. The teacher instructs the children to read all the possible answers and cross out any answer that obviously doesn't fit. Next, the students should "plug in" the remaining choices and eliminate any that are grammatically incorrect or illogical. Finally, the student should consider contextual clues in order to select the best answer. This in an example of:

a. Strategy instruction
b. Diagnostic instruction
c. Skills instruction
d. Multiple-choice instruction

31. Which of these is mainly a sign that a student has problems with reading comprehension?

a. The student has trouble recognizing words out of context.
b. The student reads laboriously, reading one word at a time.
c. The student has trouble separating the main idea from details.
d. The student has trouble relating a text to prior knowledge.

32. A student writes a fictional story about a man who struggles to work for a difficult boss. He includes the following sentences in the story:

> "John never knew which boss he would meet in the office each morning. Would it be Dr. Jekyll or Mr. Hyde?"

Which type of literary device is the student using in this example?

a. Foreshadowing
b. Irony
c. Allusion
d. Pun

33. A teacher wants to help her students develop metacognitive skills. Which guiding question can she prompt students to ask themselves while reading?

a. Who are the major and minor characters?
b. Were my predictions correct?
c. What happened first?
d. What is the theme of the story?

34. Some teachers suggest a simple visual graphic to teach younger and beginning reading students about the main idea and supporting details in nonfiction text: outline your hand on the board and have students follow suit (or give them prepared handouts with a hand outline). Label parts of the hand. Where on the hand drawing would the supporting details logically be?

a. On the thumb of the hand
b. On the fingers of the hand
c. On the palm of the hand
d. On the back of the hand

Copyright © Mometrix Media. You have been licensed one copy of this document for personal use only. Any other reproduction or redistribution is strictly prohibited. All rights reserved.
This content is provided for test preparation purposes only and does not imply an endorsement by Mometrix of any particular political, scientific, or religious point of view.

35. A teacher asks students to close their eyes while she reads a descriptive, fictional text aloud. When she is done reading, students draw pictures of the story's setting and share their pictures with the class. Which reading strategy are students practicing?

a. Predicting
b. Inferring
c. Summarizing
d. Visualizing

36. Character maps, fact and opinion charts, 5Ws charts, and webs are all examples of what?

a. Literary elements
b. Genres
c. Text features
d. Graphic organizers

37. A fifth-grade teacher is helping his students analyze how varied sentence structure contributes to the tone and mood of a text. Which of the following sentences should he use if he wants to model a complex sentence?

a. Michael ate pancakes for breakfast.
b. Michael ate breakfast and brushed his teeth.
c. Before going to school, Michael brushed his teeth.
d. Michael ate breakfast, and he brushed his teeth.

38. Which of these accurately reflects research findings related to literary genre studies?

a. Research finds experience reading various genres unrelated to writing in various genres.
b. Research finds literary analysis requires applying different strategies and skills by genre.
c. Research finds analyzing different literary genres contributes to cognitive development.
d. Research finds deeper immersion in one to two genres more important than exposure to many.

39. After students have studied metaphors for several days, a teacher wants to assess their abilities to apply their knowledge of what a metaphor is. Which assignment would be most appropriate for this purpose?

a. Underlining the metaphors in a sample text
b. Explaining what a metaphor is to a classmate
c. Writing a paragraph that includes at least two metaphors
d. Critiquing the author's use of metaphors in a poem

40. A fourth-grade teacher gives students a character chart to fill out while reading a fictional text. Students are instructed to record traits of the main character as they read. One student, Daniel, turns in a map that lists the following traits: short, has blond hair, has freckles, is a girl. Which strategy would be an appropriate next step for the teacher to focus on?

a. Analyzing character development from the beginning of the story to the end
b. Identifying the character as a protagonist or antagonist
c. Differentiating between internal and external character traits
d. Comparing and contrasting the character with a character from another book by the same author

Copyright © Mometrix Media. You have been licensed one copy of this document for personal use only. Any other reproduction or redistribution is strictly prohibited. All rights reserved.
This content is provided for test preparation purposes only and does not imply an endorsement by Mometrix of any particular political, scientific, or religious point of view.

41. Students in a sixth-grade classroom are reading a persuasive essay about the importance of recycling. Which question can the teacher ask to help students develop evaluative comprehension skills?

a. Do you agree with the author that recycling is an easy way for everyone to help the environment?
b. Which material takes longer to decompose: plastic or glass?
c. What types of materials can be recycled?
d. Who should you contact in your city if you want to help organize a recycling program?

42. Which of these is accurate about instruction that supports independent, reflective student reading?

a. Students typically write in reader response journals after both sustained silent and independent reading.
b. Student journals enable teachers to monitor reading, check comprehension, discuss, and suggest books.
c. Students typically can write in reader response journals without any modeling, prompting, or references.
d. Students should be advised to achieve a balance of 50 percent reading and 50 percent writing.

43. When can making a KWL chart help students with reading comprehension?

a. Before, during, and after students read
b. Before and during but not after reading
c. During and after but not before reading
d. Before and after but not during reading

44. Among reading materials teachers can select to promote student comprehension of nonfiction, most content-area textbooks used in public schools feature which type of writing?

a. Narrative
b. Persuasive
c. Descriptive
d. Informational

45. A teacher introduces a new book about water conservation to students and says, "As you read this book, locate three ways you can conserve water at home." What is her primary reason for this statement?

a. To encourage students to consider the author's purpose
b. To help students set a purpose for reading
c. To activate students' prior knowledge
d. To encourage students to make text-to-text connections

46. A teacher wants to help his students identify the types of nonfiction texts they are reading based on their text structures. Which keywords would students likely find in compare-and-contrast texts?

a. For example and for instance
b. Similarly and on the other hand
c. Because and as a result
d. First, next, and finally

Copyright © Mometrix Media. You have been licensed one copy of this document for personal use only. Any other reproduction or redistribution is strictly prohibited. All rights reserved.
This content is provided for test preparation purposes only and does not imply an endorsement by Mometrix of any particular political, scientific, or religious point of view.

47. Michael is a sixth-grade student who struggles to summarize fictional texts he has read. His summaries are often lengthy and include many unimportant details. Which type of graphic organizer could best help Michael develop concise summaries?

a. KWL charts
b. Semantic maps
c. Venn diagrams
d. Story maps

48. One instructional strategy to help students understand nonfiction is to teach them the elements of text structure and how to identify these by "signal" words. Among common text structures, which of these signal words indicate a descriptive structure?

a. Before, initially, secondly, next, then, last, after, finally
b. For example, in particular, specifically, and in addition
c. In comparison to, similar to, likewise, however
d. Therefore, consequently, why, because, may be due to

49. Which of the following scenarios best exemplifies an effective strategy for developing students' understanding of the author's viewpoint in informational texts?

a. Providing students with an outline template to record the main idea and supporting details in the text
b. Supplementing the text with visual aids to help with clarification, such as diagrams and illustrations
c. Assigning students to respond to a series of reflective prompts in their reader's response journals
d. Tasking students to complete a Venn diagram as they read two articles on the same topic

Refer to the following for question 50:

A third-grade teacher has students read from the following passage about the life cycle of plants and answer corresponding comprehension questions. The passage and an example of one student's work appear below.

Directions: Read the passage about the plant life cycle. Then, answer the comprehension questions below.

Just like humans and animals, plants are alive and experience many changes throughout their lifetime. During the plant life cycle, plants pass through many stages, beginning from a tiny seed to a fully grown plant that can make new seeds. Knowing about the plant life cycle is important for everyone from botanists to gardeners because it helps us understand how plants grow, how to take care of them, and what they need to thrive.

The first stage of the plant life cycle is called the seed stage. The inside of seeds has everything that a plant needs to start growing. Once seeds are planted in soil, they need water and sunlight to sprout.

The second stage in the plant life cycle is called the germination stage. During this stage, the root pushes out of the seed and begins to grow down into the soil. Above ground, you will begin to see a small young plant beginning to grow upward.

Copyright © Mometrix Media. You have been licensed one copy of this document for personal use only. Any other reproduction or redistribution is strictly prohibited. All rights reserved.
This content is provided for test preparation purposes only and does not imply an endorsement by Mometrix of any particular political, scientific, or religious point of view.

After the germination stage, plants begin the seedling stage, where they start to form leaves and grow taller. During this stage, plants must receive lots of sun, water, and nutrients from the soil so that it can grow tall and strong.

The fourth stage of the plant life cycle is called the maturity stage. During this stage, plants grow much taller and stronger, and can begin producing their own flowers and seeds.

During the fifth and last stage of the plant life cycle, the plant's seeds are dispersed and land in a new location. The plant life cycle begins again when the new seeds are planted and find a new place to grow.

Understanding the plant life cycle helps us understand the world around us, why plants are important, and what they need to survive.

Comprehension questions:

a. What is the central idea of the passage?

The life cycle of plants

b. What are the four stages of the plant life cycle?

Seed, germination, seedling, maturity, and seed spreading

c. Describe what happens in each phase of the plant life cycle.

First seeds are planted. Then they need water. They can grow both up and down. Finally they can make new seeds.

d. Why is it important to know about the life cycle of plants?

So we can grow our own food

50. Based on the information presented, which of the following strategies would likely be most effective in supporting this student's development of reading comprehension and analysis skills of informational texts?

a. Guiding the student through annotating the text as they read
b. Providing the student with a story map to record important information from the text
c. Simplifying the text to align with the student's current reading comprehension and analysis skill level
d. Prompting the student to reflect on their reading in a reader's response journal

51. A fifth-grade teacher is planning a literature unit in which students will read the novel *Charlotte's Web* over the course of several weeks. Prior to beginning the unit, the teacher assigns students to complete the following activity:

Directions: Read through each statement below. Decide whether you agree with each statement (A) or disagree (D). After reading the book, revisit each statement and mark whether your original answers were correct or incorrect.

Copyright © Mometrix Media. You have been licensed one copy of this document for personal use only. Any other reproduction or redistribution is strictly prohibited. All rights reserved.
This content is provided for test preparation purposes only and does not imply an endorsement by Mometrix of any particular political, scientific, or religious point of view.

1. Real friendship can be found despite differences. _____
2. Spending too much time around animals can be a bad thing. ____
3. Farm life is often difficult and unforgiving and is not for everyone. _____
4. Small miracles occur every day if you just look for them. ____
5. Working together helps everyone achieve their goals. ____
6. Change is often difficult and is almost never a positive thing. ____

The above assignment is an example of which pre-reading activity aimed at promoting students' literary analysis skills?

a. An anticipation guide
b. A KWL chart
c. Think-read-share
d. A story map

52. A fifth-grade teacher is planning a social studies unit on European colonization between 1400 and 1800 that will incorporate multiple informational texts. During the unit, the teacher aims to focus on developing students' ability to formulate connections between these texts. Which of the following styles of graphic organizer would be most effective in supporting students' achievement of this goal?

a. A timeline
b. A KWL chart
c. A Venn diagram
d. An outline

Oral and Written Communication

53. Which of the following purposes for writing is most likely to be included within another?

a. Description within narration
b. Narration within description
c. Persuasion within exposition
d. Exposition within narration

54. Which of the following activities best demonstrates a multisensory approach to teaching letter formation?

a. Locating words containing a certain letter in a book
b. Tracing prewritten letters on paper with a pencil
c. Identifying letters on flashcards
d. Writing letters in shaving cream

55. Which of the following represents a main difference between the conventions of spoken and written language?

a. Syntax is more relaxed in spoken language, with more flexibility in word order.
b. Body language plays a bigger role in sharing meaning in written language than in spoken language.
c. Written language tends to be less formal and more conversational in nature than spoken language.
d. Written language includes a greater mixture of fragments and complete sentences than spoken language.

Copyright © Mometrix Media. You have been licensed one copy of this document for personal use only. Any other reproduction or redistribution is strictly prohibited. All rights reserved.
This content is provided for test preparation purposes only and does not imply an endorsement by Mometrix of any particular political, scientific, or religious point of view.

Refer to the following for question 56:

A teacher has given the first paragraph of an essay to her students to analyze and discuss.

> Americans have struggled with cigarettes far too long. Until now, it has been a personal choice to smoke (or not), but the time for change is rapidly approaching. Local legislation has already begun for schools, restaurants, arenas, and other public places to be smoke-free. Years ago, cigarette smoking was presented by the media as being fashionable, even sexy. In magazines, movies, and later in television, celebrities would indulge themselves with a smoke and even be paid to endorse a brand. As recently as 1975, it was common for talk show hosts like Tom Snyder and Johnny Carson to keep a cigarette burning. Cigarette smoking in America has persisted in spite of frightening concerns like lung cancer and emphysema. Over the years, the tobacco industry has sought to diffuse strong evidence that smoking is harmful. However, the myth of "safe cigarettes," questions about nicotine addiction, and denials about the dangers of secondhand smoke have proven to be propaganda and lies.

56. The next three paragraphs in the essay will most likely address:

a. Smoking as a personal choice, changes in local legislation, and how fashionable smoking once was
b. How fashionable smoking once was, talk show hosts smoking on air, the myth of "safe cigarettes"
c. Propaganda and lies, the myth of "safe cigarettes," and how long Americans have struggled with cigarettes
d. The myth of "safe cigarettes," questions about nicotine addiction, and the dangers of secondhand smoke

57. A teacher familiarizes students with various kinds of information sources, how researchers use them, and specific conventions they follow. The teacher compares the merits, usefulness, relevance, and appropriateness of these sources relative to a class topic. How do students benefit from this instruction?

a. Direct learning about various types of source materials is the only benefit.
b. They gain deeper understanding and critical engagement via various perspectives.
c. How to build topic-related positions using evidence is not among benefits.
d. Students gain insight into selecting materials but not into evaluating them.

58. Which of these is most accurate about the research skill of formulating a research question?

a. Students typically have no problem translating their source readings into writing.
b. Teachers should begin by having students form questions on discussed concepts.
c. Teachers should begin by having students form questions from assignment topics.
d. Students may find certain graphic organizers helpful for this, but not mind-maps.

Copyright © Mometrix Media. You have been licensed one copy of this document for personal use only. Any other reproduction or redistribution is strictly prohibited. All rights reserved.
This content is provided for test preparation purposes only and does not imply an endorsement by Mometrix of any particular political, scientific, or religious point of view.

59. Students in Mr. Henderson's science class are conducting research for their science fair projects. Today, they are typing keywords into a search engine to identify sources that may be relevant for their background information. Which reading strategy should Mr. Henderson teach and practice with his students prior to this activity?

a. Skimming
b. Scanning
c. Close reading
d. Extensive reading

60. Which of these describes a student action that is characteristic of recursive writing?

a. A student writes an introduction, then the body of a work, and finishes by writing a conclusion.
b. A student brainstorms, outlines, and writes; edits it once and turns it in; and discards it after it is graded.
c. A student inserts another excellent point that just occurred to her right before publishing.
d. A student follows the five stages of writing and editing exactly, always in the prescribed sequence.

Refer to the following for question 61:

> A reading teacher is working with a student who has just moved to Texas from Korea. The child knows very few words in English. The teacher offers her a picture book of Korean folk tales. Using words and gestures, the teacher asks her to "read" one folk tale. The child "reads" the familiar tale in Korean. The teacher then writes key English words on the board and asks the child to find those words in the book. When the child finds the words, they read them together.

61. The strategy used in this situation is:

a. Useful. The child will feel more confident because the story is already familiar. She will also feel that the lesson is a conversation of sorts, and that she is communicating successfully. She will be motivated to learn the English words because they are meaningful and highly charged.
b. Useful. The teacher is learning as much as the child is. The teacher is learning about Korean culture and language, and she can apply this knowledge when teaching future Korean students.
c. Not very useful. The child needs to be exposed to as much American culture as possible. Encouraging her to remember her own culture will make her sad and will limit her curiosity about her new home.
d. Not very useful. The first things the child should learn are the letters of the alphabet and associative sounds. Only then can she begin to decipher an unfamiliar language.

62. The students enjoyed the assignment so much that the teacher suggested they select one fairy tale and modernize it without changing the basic structure. Evil kings and queens could become corrupt politicians, pumpkins could turn into Hummers, and romantic princes might reveal themselves as rock stars. The teacher believes this assignment will most effectively demonstrate to the students:

a. The importance of setting to meaning
b. The importance of characters to meaning
c. The importance of culture to meaning
d. The importance of creativity to meaning

Copyright © Mometrix Media. You have been licensed one copy of this document for personal use only. Any other reproduction or redistribution is strictly prohibited. All rights reserved.
This content is provided for test preparation purposes only and does not imply an endorsement by Mometrix of any particular political, scientific, or religious point of view.

63. Of the following, what is true about enabling students to participate actively in portfolio assessments?

a. Teachers can have students select their own work samples to reflect on their progress.
b. Teachers can give students performance criteria, but not let them help develop goals.
c. Teachers can have students create their own rubrics, but only in small or class groups.
d. Teachers can have students set realistic improvement goals but should not help them.

64. Which of the following is true about giving students effective feedback during all stages of the writing process?

a. Students are more receptive to feedback from their parents than feedback from their teachers.
b. Students explore all possibilities in their compositions when teachers treat writing as a process.
c. Students will not realize any greater benefits from feedback if teachers divide writing into steps.
d. Students are able to maintain more perspective about their work by viewing writing as a whole.

65. A fourth-grade teacher instructs students in how to locate and use information sources to answer their research questions. In this process, which of the following relates to the step of guided practice?

a. The teacher has students write research questions, find sources, take notes, and make outlines.
b. The teacher has students make outlines from their notes and classify information with support.
c. The teacher asks students how they located information and they respond, describing all steps.
d. The teacher demonstrates identifying questions, finding information, and how to categorize it.

66. A fourth-grade teacher wants to encourage students to incorporate academic language into their writing. Which of the following initial strategies would be most effective in achieving this goal?

a. Providing students with a list of sentence starters to use as a reference
b. Displaying academic vocabulary words on a class word wall
c. Conducting sentence dictation exercises that include academic vocabulary words
d. Providing students with sentence frames to guide students in their writing

67. Public speakers want to give speeches that make their audience pay attention, but they also want to give speeches whose messages are meaningful enough to remain in audience member's minds. This can best be accomplished with:

a. Simple language and stories
b. Strict logical progression
c. Sophisticated language and ideas
d. Eye contact

Copyright © Mometrix Media. You have been licensed one copy of this document for personal use only. Any other reproduction or redistribution is strictly prohibited. All rights reserved.
This content is provided for test preparation purposes only and does not imply an endorsement by Mometrix of any particular political, scientific, or religious point of view.

68. Which of these accurately reflects influences on media choices for giving presentations?

a. Combining more than one type of media is advisable.
b. Experts find it more effective to limit presentations to one medium.
c. Presenters should not let their budgets influence their choice.
d. The length of communication will not affect the media.

69. When comparing digital media to print media, which is/are the greatest digital advantage(s)?

a. Permanence
b. (c) and (d)
c. Versatility
d. Flexibility

70. Of the following criteria for critically evaluating how effective an informational text author's methods of appealing to the reading audience are, which is related to whether readers believed the author, and why they did or did not?

a. Clarity
b. Accuracy
c. Cohesion
d. Credibility

71. Which of the following can the writer determine without considering the audience?

a. Purpose
b. Structure
c. Word choice
d. Amount of research

72. In the steps that a reader can follow to evaluate an informational text writer's arguments, which should come first?

a. Identifying the conclusion the argument makes
b. Judging the validity or supportiveness of premises
c. Clarifying premises or reasons with paraphrases
d. Identifying the supporting premises or reasons

73. Common standards for middle school grades include evaluating textual arguments and claims. Within this standard, which of the following is an element applying uniquely to the eighth grade?

a. Tracing/delineating and evaluating argument and specific claims in a text
b. Distinguishing claims supported by evidence and reasons versus being unsupported
c. Assessing whether reasoning is sound and evidence is relevant and sufficient
d. Recognizing whether some evidence that has been introduced is irrelevant

74. Suppose a written or spoken argument's claim is that community colleges in your state have recently had their budgets cut. Which of these would be sufficient evidence to prove this claim?

a. Citing the largest budget cut at one college
b. Citing two prominent examples of the cuts
c. Citing examples from 15 of the 34 community colleges in the state
d. Citing specific cut amounts at all 34 colleges

Copyright © Mometrix Media. You have been licensed one copy of this document for personal use only. Any other reproduction or redistribution is strictly prohibited. All rights reserved.
This content is provided for test preparation purposes only and does not imply an endorsement by Mometrix of any particular political, scientific, or religious point of view.

Educating All Learners and Professional Practice

75. What is one benefit of using a rubric over other types of assessment techniques?

a. Rubrics break down overall scores by criteria, allowing students to see their strengths and weaknesses.
b. Rubrics allow students to track their progress over time.
c. Rubrics help students see how they did in comparison with their peers.
d. Rubrics help identify the types of reading miscues students are making so teachers can provide targeted instruction.

76. Which of these is most accurate about the failure of some reading curriculum designs?

a. Curriculum designs fail when their components fail, rather than being incompatible.
b. An essential element of curriculum design is provision for continuous improvement.
c. Curriculum designs fail due to component incompatibility, not to component failure.
d. Personnel not wanting to implement or misunderstanding a design cause its failure.

77. Which instructional strategy is most closely related to and is a key component of schema theory?

a. Summarizing
b. Activating prior knowledge
c. Identifying main idea
d. Recognizing story elements

78. An ELL is having difficulties comprehending a science textbook because it contains many unknown vocabulary words with few accompanying visuals. Which instructional strategy would most likely assist the student with this difficulty?

a. Reading the textbook aloud to him rather than asking him to read it independently
b. Supplying him with an audio version of the textbook
c. Providing him with a printed outline of each chapter's main points
d. Giving him access to a multimedia version of the textbook to view on his computer

79. Which of the following teacher actions would most effectively encourage reading development in students' home environments?

a. Reminding students to read with their parents each day
b. Sending home a weekly update listing the phonics skills the class practiced
c. Sending home a list of weekly spelling words for students to memorize
d. Sending home leveled texts for students to read with family members

80. Relative to the influences of cultural contexts on language development, which of these is true about various world cultures and languages?

a. All cultures have social conventions and body language as well as spoken, written, or signed language.
b. All cultures have spoken but not necessarily written language.
c. All cultures have written but not necessarily spoken language.
d. All cultures have only social conventions and body language.

Copyright © Mometrix Media. You have been licensed one copy of this document for personal use only. Any other reproduction or redistribution is strictly prohibited. All rights reserved.
This content is provided for test preparation purposes only and does not imply an endorsement by Mometrix of any particular political, scientific, or religious point of view.

81. Compared with whole-class instruction, small-group instruction is particularly useful for which of the following?

a. Teach main ideas or strategic integration
b. Instruction in rhyming and onsets
c. Use read-alouds for oral practice
d. Diagnose reading difficulties and design reading interventions

82. Regarding alternative lesson structures for differentiating reading instruction, for which of these should a teacher use skills-focused lessons rather than guided reading lessons?

a. For monitoring how well students apply skills to reading text
b. For helping students in mastering comprehension strategies
c. For helping students discuss the meaning of texts they read
d. For supporting students in using reading comprehension skills

83. Of the following, which kind of learning disability would have the most direct impact on a student's reading instruction?

a. An expressive language disorder
b. A receptive language disorder
c. An articulation disorder
d. A movement disorder

84. Among the following, which is an indicator of reliability in a reading assessment instrument?

a. The test measures the reading skill it specifically claims to measure.
b. The test measures the reading skill through open-ended questions.
c. The test measures the reading skill using a few very focused items.
d. The test measures the reading skill consistently over repeated uses.

85. Which of these have researchers found about the relationship of family involvement in education to student outcomes?

a. Students with families involved in their learning get higher grades, take more advanced classes, have higher graduation rates, and are more likely to attend postsecondary education.
b. Students perform their best academically when their parents concentrate on adopting one specific major role in their learning, like participating in school events and activities.
c. Students whose families actively support their learning have better attendance and attitudes toward school, but do not demonstrate any better behavior while they are there.
d. Students from diverse backgrounds feel more comfortable in school as a result of school-family collaboration to bridge cultural gaps, but are not found to perform better academically.

86. Relative to stakeholder concerns with a school reading program, what is true about conflict resolution?

a. Conflict is always negative; thus, it can and should be avoided.
b. Conflict resolution processes are unrelated to self-knowledge.
c. Conflict is an opportunity for social change and moral growth.
d. Conflict is ubiquitous, yet it is analyzed more but described less.

Copyright © Mometrix Media. You have been licensed one copy of this document for personal use only. Any other reproduction or redistribution is strictly prohibited. All rights reserved.
This content is provided for test preparation purposes only and does not imply an endorsement by Mometrix of any particular political, scientific, or religious point of view.

87. Based on assessment findings, a teacher introduces her students to graphic organizers to help them understand concepts. Which of the following is NOT a way graphic organizers help students?

a. They present concepts in visual form.
b. They convert the verbal to numerical.
c. They help students compare, contrast, separate, and group concepts.
d. They enable students to classify or categorize concepts.

88. Researchers have identified which of the following about norm-referenced reading tests?

a. They are better for assessing abstract cognitive levels.
b. They are better for assessing in homogeneous groups.
c. They are better for assessing narrow ranges of ability.
d. They are better for assessing limited outcome ranges.

89. The National Education Association (NEA) identifies a number of strategies for schools to form effective family and community partnerships. For example, one is to use culturally appropriate outreach targeting the concerns of high-needs students, schools, and communities. What is another strategy?

a. Schools take time to build one-to-one family-educator relationships, discuss, and agree to optimal collaboration for students.
b. Schools take care not to set or communicate high or rigorous expectations that intimidate at-risk or marginal students.
c. Schools require teachers and educational support professionals to overcome barriers of culture, class, and language.
d. Schools establish community connections to offer students relevant, hands-on learning, not for community service.

90. A fourth-grade teacher is planning a reader's theater activity to promote prosodic reading skills and reading fluency among students. Small groups will be assigned by proficiency levels, and students will be assigned to act out a familiar play suited to their abilities. Throughout the week, students will have the opportunity to practice their play and will be encouraged to focus on expression, intonation, tone, and inflection. Which of the following additional strategies could the teacher incorporate to further modify the activity to align with varying reading fluency levels?

a. Instructing students to read the play independently before beginning the reader's theater activity to familiarize them with the text
b. Allowing students to select their preferred roles within the play to enhance engagement and confidence in reading
c. Having students complete self-assessment activities after each practice session to reflect on their progress
d. Implementing guided reading sessions with each group to support struggling readers in mastering their lines and improving overall comprehension and fluency

Copyright © Mometrix Media. You have been licensed one copy of this document for personal use only. Any other reproduction or redistribution is strictly prohibited. All rights reserved.
This content is provided for test preparation purposes only and does not imply an endorsement by Mometrix of any particular political, scientific, or religious point of view.

Answer Key and Explanations for Test #1

Foundations of Reading

1. C: Formal assessments are administered and scored in a standardized fashion, so scoring is objective. Therefore, a standardized state reading test is an example of a formal reading assessment because all students take the test under the same conditions, and the tests should all be scored in the same way. The remaining options are situation dependent and not administered in a standardized manner. Additionally, various teachers may evaluate students differently, with results therefore being subjective.

2. D: Informal Reading Inventories assess students in multiple areas of reading performance, including decoding, comprehension, recall, and fluency. The results can be used to identify areas in need of improvement, group students for targeted reading instruction, and match students with appropriate texts. They do not record texts students have read throughout the year, which can be done using reading logs, nor do they identify areas of student interest. Other assessment and screening tools exist to determine which reading behaviors and skills students have already learned prior to entering school.

3. C: Finger-pointing is normal for beginning readers, even into second grade (A); adults should not interfere with pointing. Giving young children "witch fingers," feathers, and other available, recycled, or homemade pointers is fine. These are not crutches (B); they are simply finger substitutes that are creative, fun, and keep book pages clean with younger readers. However, when older students finger-point, it can indicate reading struggles and interfere with reading fluency (C). Having students turn bookmarks or popsicle sticks sideways to mark each line of text helps them transition past finger-pointing (D).

4. C: Ongoing informal assessments include any actions the teacher takes to check for students' comprehension of the material, even so small as to ask for classroom discussion about a story to gauge how well the class as a whole understands the content. Because ongoing informal assessments are so casual, they tend to be faster and easier for all students to complete, and the students may be unaware that they are even being assessed. This lack of pressure, combined with the opportunity to ask questions tailored to individual student, gives the teacher a great opportunity to assess, provide individualized instruction, and motivate students at the same time.

Informal assessments tend to better reflect an English language learner's (ELL) content knowledge than formal tests because formal tests present several issues with testing reliability and validity and may not accurately gauge content knowledge alone. For instance, a science or mathematics test may not present any linguistic difficulties to a native English speaker, and will not interfere with the test's ability to gauge their content knowledge. For an ELL, however, a student may encounter linguistic barriers that interfere with their comprehension or speed in taking a test and consequently interferes with the accurate measurement of their understanding of the subject matter.

Informal assessments do tend to hold lower weight in grades than formal tests because they are too individualized and casual to provide a full picture of progress toward comprehension of the curriculum. Despite this, informal assessments are arguably more important than formal assessments because they are so effective for making flexible adjustments to instruction to better meet the needs of the student and the class as a whole.

Copyright © Mometrix Media. You have been licensed one copy of this document for personal use only. Any other reproduction or redistribution is strictly prohibited. All rights reserved.
This content is provided for test preparation purposes only and does not imply an endorsement by Mometrix of any particular political, scientific, or religious point of view.

5. A: Cognates are words in different languages that share the same roots, such as the English word *conflict* and the Spanish word *conflicto*. If students know the meanings of the words in their native languages, they can apply that knowledge to determine the meanings of the English words. Realia are everyday objects that provide visual representations of words, also contributing to vocabulary development. While recognizing known parts in cognates can assist students with decoding new words quickly, it is less likely to assist with prosody. Phonological and phonemic awareness have to do with identifying and manipulating sounds in words rather than identifying word meanings or related spelling patterns.

6. B: Consonant blend refers to a group of consonants in which each letter represents a separate sound.

7. B: Closed syllables are those that end with a consonant. *At, dog, spit, duck,* and *pluck* are all examples of closed syllables.

8. D: Implicit phonics instruction uses a whole-to-part approach, with students reading whole texts rather than starting with isolated phonemes. Students learn to recognize whole words by sight. Through analyzing and comparing words, they then discover phonics and spelling patterns. A benefit is that students read authentic texts and learn in a meaningful context rather than practicing skills in isolation. However, research has shown that explicit phonics instruction, which progresses from part to whole, leads to stronger decoding, spelling, and comprehension skills.

9. D: A free morpheme, also known as a base word, can stand alone as a word. In choice D, *friend* is a free morpheme. An affix can be either a prefix or a suffix, and *friendless* has one suffix, *-less*. Choice A has a prefix, *un*; a free morpheme, *help*; and a suffix, *-ful*. Choice B has a prefix, *pre-*; a free morpheme, *view*; and a suffix, *-ing*. *Truck* only has a free morpheme and no affixes.

10. A: While all of these options are important and beneficial for reading development, research has indicated that phonemic awareness is one of the strongest predictors of early reading success. Understanding that words are made up of individual sounds assists with learning the letter/sound relationships in phonics. These relationships are used to decode words.

11. C: Phonological awareness skills typically progress in a similar manner. The ability to rhyme often develops first, as it is considered the simplest skill. Later, children develop the ability to break words into syllables, which is usually followed by the ability to manipulate onsets and rimes. Phoneme isolation and other phonemic awareness skills typically develop last, as they are the most complex.

12. B: On a continuum, the simplest level of phonological awareness is represented by being able to recognize and produce rhymes in songs, and show understanding that sentences contain individual words by segmenting them (D). Segmenting words into syllables and blending syllables into words (A) represents a more complex level around the middle of the continuum. A higher level of complexity is segmenting words into onsets and rimes and blending onsets and rimes into words (C). The highest level is phonemic awareness, i.e., understanding that words contain individual phonemes and being able to manipulate (blend, segment, delete, substitute) these (B).

13. B: R-controlled vowels appear before the letter *r* in a word. The *r* changes the sound of the vowel. In the other options, the *r* comes before the vowel, and the vowel sound is not changed.

14. D: In choice D, the student read the sentence correctly, except for changing *chases* to *chased*. *Chased* still sounds right in the sentence, indicating that the student was using structural, or syntactic, cues to decode the word. In choice A, the student replaced *stick* with *branch*. *Branch*

Copyright © Mometrix Media. You have been licensed one copy of this document for personal use only. Any other reproduction or redistribution is strictly prohibited. All rights reserved.
This content is provided for test preparation purposes only and does not imply an endorsement by Mometrix of any particular political, scientific, or religious point of view.

makes sense in the sentence, and it is not visually similar to the existing word. Choice B demonstrates an insertion, as the student added the word *big*. Choice C demonstrates a visual error, as the student replaced *furry* with *fuzzy*. Both words are visually similar.

15. C: Motivation, i.e., how interested students are in reading and in what ways (e.g., genres, subject matter, reading levels, etc.), is a psychological factor that influences not only whether or how much students read but also their comprehension. Attention (A) is a prerequisite for comprehension, problems with visual and auditory perception (C) can cause reading problems, and working memory (D) is required for word decoding and reading comprehension. Unlike motivation, these three are all cognitive factors.

16. B: Academic vocabulary refers to words typically used in school conversations and texts. They are words related to the processes and concepts taught in multiple subject areas. Listening vocabulary refers to words that a person can understand when heard aloud. Children can often understand words that they hear before using them in their own speech and writing. Receptive vocabulary refers to all of the words that a person can understand when encountered in speech or writing. Expressive vocabulary refers to all of the words that a person can correctly use in his or her own speech or writing.

17. A: Context skills, i.e., the strategies a student uses to acquire incidental vocabulary learning by using context clues (e.g., surrounding words, illustrations, titles, captions, etc.), represent an implicit learning strategy. The other answer choices are all explicit instructional strategies. Root analysis (B) involves identifying common Greek and Latin roots in new words to inform their meanings. Word maps (C) are graphic organizers used to identify a word's category, qualities, and examples to inform comprehension. Using keywords or word clues (e.g., images, examples, or definition parts) (D) helps students to figure out vocabulary words without needing to memorize definitions before reading.

18. C: This sentence contains the word *firm*, which is an antonym for *tentative*. This antonym, along with the word *unlike*, help the reader determine that *tentative* means not firm. There are no synonyms, or words that mean the same, for *tentative* in the sentence. There are also no definitions for the word. Inference clues give hints about the word's meaning without explicitly listing a synonym, antonym, or definition. No such inference clues are present.

19. D: When students participate in kinesthetic activities, they are physically engaged in the learning process. These activities involve movement, such as hopping along the sight words written in chalk. While the other activities can also be used to practice sight words and may involve tactile experiences, they involve less movement and physical activity than hopping.

20. A: Tier-two vocabulary words are high-frequency and challenging words that hold a lot of meaning within the text. Because they appear frequently, not knowing their meanings can affect comprehension in multiple texts. High-frequency, concrete nouns are tier-one words. These are usually learned through everyday interactions and do not require explicit instruction. Domain-specific words are tier-three words. While it is beneficial for students to learn and use these words in some academic and professional contexts, they are unlikely to appear in everyday texts. Student-selected words may be used to generate interest in the topic and help students become actively involved in their learning. However, there is no guarantee that students will choose high-frequency words.

21. D: Teacher-directed reading is one method of instructing the whole class together. In this method, the teacher often has a passage or patterned sentences that the teacher will use to model

Copyright © Mometrix Media. You have been licensed one copy of this document for personal use only. Any other reproduction or redistribution is strictly prohibited. All rights reserved.
This content is provided for test preparation purposes only and does not imply an endorsement by Mometrix of any particular political, scientific, or religious point of view.

reading practices to the class. In the "pre-reading" phase, the teacher should give the students supportive information, such as the title, topic, or new key words that the student will encounter. In the "during reading" phase, the teacher will model a sentence, then ask the class to repeat the sentence, following along with the modeled decoding and tracking techniques. In the "after reading" phase, the teacher should ask the students to apply and practice this pattern more independently on their own to gain experience decoding and tracking. In this method, the "during reading" phase takes place actively as a class, which is not represented by the other choices. Independent or partner practice usually takes place in the "after reading" phase of this type of activity.

22. B: Closed syllables, i.e., those ending in a consonant and typically preceded by a short vowel sound (e.g., *fabric, rabbit*), are the syllable pattern type used most often, so they should be taught first, before open (A) or other syllable types. To teach from simpler to more complex, instruction in decoding multisyllabic words should also teach strategies for syllabication divisions after introducing multisyllabic words, not before (C). Also, teachers should teach spelling generalizations based on syllable pattern types, not vice versa (D).

23. B: This trend has merit in the fact that it allows students to use the resources they already have instead of artificially suppressing the use of technology. Choice A is incorrect because, while not all students have phones, many do. Smartphones are among the most popular, ubiquitous, convenient, and mobile of devices that individuals use. Over time, smartphones have become increasingly prevalent, demonstrating that they are not considered too expensive in general. While it is unreasonable to expect all students to have their own phones, if device usage becomes fully integrated into curriculum, those who do not have access to a phone could be supplied by the school, in a similar fashion to classroom tablets or computers. Choice C is incorrect because device usage plays a big role in instruction, privacy, and safety for students. It is crucial to have acceptable use policies in place for technology. The scenario does not describe the school policy, but teachers who want to integrate technology into instruction must follow district and campus policies to ensure the legality of the practice and safety of the students. Choice D is incorrect as student privacy is inherently tied to the use of personal devices. A teacher should be able to give guidance to students on how to use any appropriate technology, and would ideally have a direct line of communication about classwork, but teachers should not expect to have complete access to students' personal devices.

24. C: Researchers have found that not all children benefit from instruction in phonological awareness (A), even though most children do. Children at risk for speech or language delays do not benefit most (B); studies providing this instruction have shown that almost one-third of at-risk children realized little or no improvement. But the benefits are not limited to children with normal language development (D), either. Some of these researchers have concluded the instruction must be more intensive or explicit for at-risk students.

25. C: Final blending individually identifies and pronounces each phoneme in a word before blending them. This helps teachers identify specific problem areas: some students may give the wrong sound for a letter; others may identify letter-sounds correctly without blending (e.g., pronouncing /sa/ as "suh-ah," not "sah"). Successive blending (A) pronounces individual phonemes sequentially; teachers first prolong (e.g., "ssssuuuunnnn"), then gradually shorten prolonged phonemes ("sssuuunnn," "ssuunn," "sun"). Teachers help students eventually transition from blending aloud to silent blending (B). Line blending (D) cumulatively reviews word sets and sentences already taught until students can blend independently.

26. C: In the five established spelling development stages, in Stage 1 (A) children learn the difference between drawing and writing, letter formation, writing directionality, and some letter-

Copyright © Mometrix Media. You have been licensed one copy of this document for personal use only. Any other reproduction or redistribution is strictly prohibited. All rights reserved.
This content is provided for test preparation purposes only and does not imply an endorsement by Mometrix of any particular political, scientific, or religious point of view.

sound correspondences, but not the alphabetic principle. In Stage 3 (B), they learn long and r-controlled vowel spelling patterns, more advanced consonant patterns, diphthongs, and other less familiar vowel patterns. In Stage 2 (C), they learn the alphabetic principle, i.e., that letters represent corresponding speech sounds, and they also learn consonant and short vowel sounds, consonant blends, and digraphs. In Stage 4 (D), they learn grammatical suffixes and rules, syllabication, and homophones.

27. D: The best way for teachers to promote language, literacy, and reading development is to integrate oral language, written language, modeling, and interaction into classroom activities in a variety of interactive settings. Choices A, B, and C all call upon one aspect, but do not include any interactive steps. Choice D is the best option because it calls upon interaction and includes reading and writing, as well as the potential for oral language skills.

28. B: Understanding the concepts of onset and rime is essential to developing word recognition skills, vocabulary acquisition, and ultimately, reading fluency. Use of word families is a highly effective strategy for introducing this concept to young readers, at it helps them to identify patterns, recognize words within the same family, and comprehend how changing the onset creates new words. To further reinforce this concept, it is important to provide students with ample opportunities to practice and manipulate new vocabulary. One effective strategy for achieving this includes implementing word-building activities using magnetic letter tiles. For example, in the given scenario, the teacher would provide students with letter tiles based on the displayed chart and the *-all* word family. This kinesthetic approach allows students to physically manipulate the onset and rime of new vocabulary words, thus strengthening their understanding and building foundational reading fluency skills.

29. A: Encountering new academic vocabulary can pose a significant challenge for young children, particularly as they reach upper elementary school where language becomes increasingly complex. As such, implementing strategies to help students decipher unfamiliar terms is essential in fostering academic language acquisition and reading fluency skills. Encouraging students to utilize context clues when encountering unfamiliar vocabulary is an effective strategy for helping them derive meaning. One such strategy involves prompting students to refer to pictures or illustrations in a text to determine the meaning of an unfamiliar word. Visual images in a text provide students with contextual information, including tone, setting, actions, or objects associated with a new word, thus allowing them to infer meaning and attach a tangible example to the unfamiliar vocabulary. By encouraging students to refer to images in a text as context clues, teachers can promote improved comprehension and retention of academic language. Using the text surrounding an unknown word is also a strategy students can employ when encountering new words. Often, the context of a sentence can be enough for the student to guess the meaning of the word. This strategy becomes especially useful in texts without pictures.

Text Comprehension and Analysis

30. A: Strategic instruction involves teaching a methodic approach to solving a reading problem. It consists of strategies done in steps which aid the reader in eliminating incorrect responses.

31. C: When a student has trouble recognizing words out of context (A), this is mainly a sign that the student has problems with decoding words, as is slow, laborious oral reading (B). Having trouble differentiating main ideas or important information from minor details (C) in text is mainly a sign that the student has problems with reading comprehension. Having trouble relating text to his or her own existing knowledge (D) often reflects difficulty using background knowledge, which

Copyright © Mometrix Media. You have been licensed one copy of this document for personal use only. Any other reproduction or redistribution is strictly prohibited. All rights reserved.
This content is provided for test preparation purposes only and does not imply an endorsement by Mometrix of any particular political, scientific, or religious point of view.

can influence comprehension but is conceptually distinct from basic comprehension skills such as identifying main ideas.

32. C: Allusion is a literary device where references are made to commonly known people or events without describing them explicitly. In this example, readers are expected to understand that the reference to Dr. Jekyll and Mr. Hyde means that the employee never knows whether his boss will be pleasant or difficult each day. Foreshadowing refers to clues in the text that hint at future events. Irony is used to signify that something is the opposite of what is expected. Puns are a type of humorous wordplay involving words that have multiple meanings.

33. B: Metacognition refers to thinking about one's own thinking. Proficient readers use metacognitive skills to self-monitor their own understanding and make corrections when necessary. Making predictions, and then later assessing and revising them if necessary, demonstrates use of metacognitive skills. The other options require students to recall and/or analyze information, but they do not ask students to reflect on their own thinking.

34. B: In the hand outline instructional strategy (cf. Cox, 2009), the thumb (A) represents the topic sentence. This is logical as the hand has only one thumb, and it is a small but important part. The palm (C) represents the main idea, which is logical since it is a single, important, and larger part. The back of the hand (D) is not used, since a two-dimensional drawing would require drawing two hands or turning the paper over. The fingers (B) represent the supporting details, a logical match because there are multiple fingers on a hand and they are smaller than the palm.

35. D: When readers visualize, they use the clues and details in the stories to form mental pictures in their minds. When students draw a setting based on how they imagined it from the description in the story, they are visualizing. Predicting refers to making guesses about the text before reading. Inferring refers to using clues in the story to determine the meaning when it is not explicitly stated. Summarizing refers to retelling the main events of the story.

36. D: Character maps, fact and opinion charts, 5Ws charts, and webs are all examples of graphic organizers, which are used to help students organize and visualize information, concepts, and relationships. Literary elements are components of fictional stories, such as characters and settings. Genres are categories of texts, such as biographies and fairy tales. Text features are parts of nonfiction texts, such as headings and graphics, that are used to organize the text and provide additional information.

37. C: A complex sentence has at least one dependent and one independent clause. A dependent clause cannot stand alone as a sentence, while an independent clause can. In choice C, the dependent clause is, "Before going to school"; while the independent clause is, "Michael brushed his teeth." Choice A is a simple sentence containing one independent clause. Choice B is a sentence with a compound predicate. Choice D is a compound sentence, meaning it contains two or more independent clauses joined by a coordinating conjunction or semicolon.

38. C: As the National Council of Teachers of English (NCTE) and International Literacy Association (ILA) point out, multiple researchers have found that the more experience students acquire with reading various literary genres, the more success they realize with writing in various genres (A). Experts find that analyzing various literary genres enables students to apply similar, not different (B), strategies and skills (e.g., identifying themes) across genres, promoting cognitive development (C). Genre studies expose students to many genres, which is more important than in-depth study of only one or two (D).

Copyright © Mometrix Media. You have been licensed one copy of this document for personal use only. Any other reproduction or redistribution is strictly prohibited. All rights reserved.
This content is provided for test preparation purposes only and does not imply an endorsement by Mometrix of any particular political, scientific, or religious point of view.

39. C: Writing their own examples of metaphors requires students to apply their knowledge. Identifying and underlining metaphors assesses the comprehension level of Bloom's taxonomy, and defining a metaphor assesses the knowledge level. Critiquing the author's use of metaphors assesses the evaluation level.

40. C: Daniel has identified only external character traits, or traits related to the character's appearance. He has not identified any internal traits, or traits related to the character's thoughts, feelings, words, or actions. An appropriate next step would be to help Daniel differentiate between the two types of traits and find examples of each in the text. The remaining options would require Daniel to identify internal traits using textual evidence. For example, it would be difficult to describe how the character has changed throughout the story without using any internal traits to describe her at different points in the story. Similarly, it would be difficult to label the role she plays or compare her with other characters without using any internal traits to support the responses.

41. A: Evaluative questions require readers to form opinions or judgements based on the text. Asking if readers agree with something the author stated is an evaluative question. The remaining questions ask students to recall information only.

42. B: Students reflect in reader response journals after independent, not sustained silent, reading (A). Teachers can use journals to monitor student reading, check comprehension, discuss texts, and suggest additional books (B). Not all students know how to respond to text by writing. Teachers should initially model the process, including prompts, and post lists of these, model methods for generating personal topics without prompts through the year, and give students lists of these for reference (C) to keep in their journals. Teachers should advise students to read about 80 percent of the time and write about 20 percent of the time (D).

43. A: A KWL chart is a type of graphic organizer that teachers can have students make to assist them with reading comprehension. K stands for *know*: before reading, students record what they already know about the subject of a text. W stands for *want*: before and during reading, students record what they want to know about the subject. L stands for *learned*: after reading, students record what they learned from reading the text.

44. D: Although some history textbooks may use narrative (A) writing to make historical events more interesting by telling a story, these are not in the majority. Persuasive (B) writing seeks to convince readers to agree with the author's position; most content-area textbooks used in public schools present information more objectively. Descriptive (C) writing seeks to convey a vivid impression of something by providing sensory details so readers feel they are experiencing it; most content-area textbooks are more factual. The majority of school content textbooks use informational (D) writing to impart knowledge.

45. B: By assigning students a task that will require them to focus on key pieces of information in the text, the teacher is helping students set a purpose for reading. She is not asking the students why the author wrote the book, which would encourage them to consider the author's purpose. Choice C is incorrect because she did not ask students what they already know about the topic of water conservation. Choice D is incorrect because she did not ask students to compare or contrast this text with any other texts they have read.

46. B: The keywords in choice B are used to signal how two or more items are the same and different, which is the purpose of compare-and-contrast texts. The keywords in choice A would likely be found in descriptive texts. The keywords in choice C would likely be found in cause-and-effect texts. The keywords in choice D would likely be found in sequential texts.

Copyright © Mometrix Media. You have been licensed one copy of this document for personal use only. Any other reproduction or redistribution is strictly prohibited. All rights reserved.
This content is provided for test preparation purposes only and does not imply an endorsement by Mometrix of any particular political, scientific, or religious point of view.

47. D: A story map helps students identify the main events of a fictional story, along with the conflict and resolution. Listing the main events can assist Michael with writing a concise summary. A KWL chart helps students identify what they know, want to know, and learned about a topic. A semantic map contains a word or concept in the center of a diagram, with related words or phrases branching off from the middle. It is useful for helping students identify relationships between concepts. A Venn diagram helps students compare and contrast two or more things.

48. B: The signal words in (A) indicate a sequential, chronological text structure. The signal words in (B) indicate a descriptive text structure. The signal words in (C) indicate a comparison-contrast text structure. The signal words in (D) indicate a cause-and-effect text structure.

49. D: Understanding the author's viewpoint is an important part of comprehending and analyzing informational texts, as it enables readers to think critically about the author's intent, perspective, and potential biases. Having students complete a Venn diagram as they read two articles about the same topic is an effective strategy for demonstrating variances in perspective among authors. Through this approach, students can focus their attention on key details as they read and identify similarities and differences in opinion, tone, language, and content with a graphic organizer as a visual aid. This will allow students to recognize how different perspectives can impact the presentation of material in an informational text, thus strengthening their ability to critically analyze and comprehend their reading on a deeper level.

50. A: Teaching students to actively engage with informational texts is necessary for developing their ability to recognize and recall key details that support the main idea, thus fostering deeper analysis and comprehension. Students that struggle to do so will likely require targeted support to improve upon their skills in this area. One effective approach involves guiding these students through annotating the text as they engage in reading. This may include strategies such as having students write notes or questions in the margins, highlighting key points and main ideas, or using sticky notes to mark important information. This approach fosters a close reading of the text, thus promoting meaningful interaction with it and focusing students' attention on essential details. By guiding the student in the given scenario through the process of text annotation, this teacher can effectively support their development of reading comprehension and analysis skills in relation to informational texts.

51. A: An integral aspect of developing students' reading comprehension and literary analysis skills involves implementing effective pre-reading strategies. Doing so enhances student engagement in reading by calling upon prior knowledge and fostering personal connections. Furthermore, pre-reading activities prompt students to focus on specific aspects of a text, such as characters, setting, plot, themes, and literary techniques, thus fostering their ability to understand complex works of literature, analyze key elements, and employ critical thinking skills to consider the author's deeper implications. Anticipation guides are a highly effective pre-reading strategy for increasing comprehension and analysis skills. This versatile activity can be differentiated to align with a variety of texts across genres. When reading works of literature, anticipation guides typically prompt students to agree or disagree with a series of statements related to a given text, as well as formulate predictions prior to engaging in reading. This activity establishes a purpose for reading, directs students' attention to specific components of the text, and encourages them to think critically as they read for increased overall engagement. By implementing anticipation guides, educators can encourage students to interact meaningfully with a text and reflect upon their original thoughts after reading, thus strengthening reading comprehension and literary analysis skills.

Copyright © Mometrix Media. You have been licensed one copy of this document for personal use only. Any other reproduction or redistribution is strictly prohibited. All rights reserved.
This content is provided for test preparation purposes only and does not imply an endorsement by Mometrix of any particular political, scientific, or religious point of view.

52. C: Facilitating identification and analysis of similarities and differences between texts is beneficial for helping students make connections between them. Such connections allow students to consider various perspectives, identify common elements, and synthesize information, thus strengthening their overall understanding of a concept. In the given scenario, providing students with a Venn diagram to compare and contrast texts focused on European colonization would be most suitable in supporting their development of this skill. This format will allow students to visually identify and analyze both common and distinct components of the texts, thus promoting critical thinking and a deeper understanding of the time period.

Oral and Written Communication

53. A: Descriptive writing, which is to "paint a picture" in words making something seem real to a reader's imagination, is more often included within narrative writing (A), i.e., storytelling like novels, short stories, biographies, etc. Other than certain character sketches, photo captions, ads, etc., most works are not entirely descriptive. Also, telling a story (like an anecdote) in the middle of descriptive writing could disrupt the description, since these have different purposes (B). Exposition is to inform or explain, so it typically does not include persuasive writing (C). Since narration's purpose is storytelling, it is less likely to include exposition (D).

54. D: While all of these options can assist students with learning letter formation, writing letters in shaving cream best represents a multisensory approach. It involves movement, touch, and sight.

55. A: Spoken language is generally less formal and more conversational in tone than written language. As a result, syntax is more relaxed, and there is greater flexibility in word order. Spoken language also tends to contain a mixture of sentences and fragments. For example, a typical conversation among friends may contain several shifts between speakers, along with brief comments and replies rather than fully developed sentences. Body language plays a greater role in spoken language, as it can either affirm or contradict the meaning of the spoken words. For example, if a person says they are looking forward to something, yet they are frowning and avoiding eye contact, the recipient of the message may not believe the speaker is sincere.

56. D: The next three paragraphs will likely address the myth of "safe cigarettes," questions about nicotine addiction, and the dangers of secondhand smoke. These three foci are presented in the thesis statement in this order and will be fleshed out in the following three paragraphs as the body of the essay.

57. B: Students gain deeper understanding and critical engagement by being exposed to various perspectives and learning to evaluate and compare sources relative to a topic. A is incorrect because it claims that direct learning about source types is the only benefit, which ignores the critical thinking benefits that students also gain. C is incorrect because the statement "how to build topic-related positions using evidence is not among benefits" is false; students do learn to construct evidence-based positions. D is incorrect because students gain insight into both selecting and evaluating sources, not just selection as implied by the option.

58. C: Many students lack understanding of connecting reading to writing on research topics (A). Teachers can help them learn to formulate research questions as the first writing step through early activities like converting assignment topics into core questions and related subordinate questions (C) to approach sources. Once students have enough practice, in later years, teachers can lead class discussions of concepts and have students formulate research questions about these (B). One graphic organizer students often find helps organize ideas and arguments are mind-maps (D), with the question central, and pro and con arguments and supporting references as branches.

Copyright © Mometrix Media. You have been licensed one copy of this document for personal use only. Any other reproduction or redistribution is strictly prohibited. All rights reserved.
This content is provided for test preparation purposes only and does not imply an endorsement by Mometrix of any particular political, scientific, or religious point of view.

59. A: When readers skim, they look through a text quickly to determine what it is mostly about. Skimming would help the students quickly identify which sites listed in the search results are closely related to the science fair topics and warrant further, deeper reading. Scanning involves reading quickly to pick out certain pieces of information from a text, such as a specific fact or date. Close reading involves rereading a text multiple times while analyzing different layers each time. Extensive reading refers to students selecting books that are enjoyable and easy to read independently, which helps increase reading rate and fluency.

60. C: When a student simply writes the parts of a composition in sequence (A), this is not recursive. Recursive writing repeats various parts of composition at any or all times during the process, including repeating some parts multiple times as needed. Thus brainstorming, outlining, writing, editing once, turning work in, and discarding it after it is graded (B) is not recursive. Always rigidly following the five stages (pre-writing, drafting, revising, editing, publishing) in sequence (D) precludes recursion. One example of recursive writing is when a student inserts another excellent point he or she suddenly thought of right before publishing (C).

61. A: The child will feel more confident because the story is already familiar, so this strategy is useful. She will also feel that the lesson is a conversation of sorts, and that she is communicating successfully. She will be motivated to learn the English words because they are meaningful and highly charged. As a newly arrived immigrant, the child feels overwhelmed. Presenting her with a book of folk tales from her country tells her that she needn't lose her culture in order to function in this one. It also comforts her by reminding her that her past and present are linked. Allowing her to speak in Korean helps her express herself without fear of judgment or failure. Presenting her with an English vocabulary that is meaningful ensures that she will eagerly embrace these words, her first words in her new language.

62. C: Authors make thousands of decisions in the act of writing: what point of view to take, how much weight to give an event, what to reveal about a character, what words will most effectively express the writer's intention, and more. While many of these decisions are consciously artistic choices, some are unconscious and imbedded in the cultural expectations of time and place in which the author has lived. To understand a text to the fullest degree possible, it is necessary to read it with an eye to the cultural framework it came from.

63. A: One way teachers can enable active student participation in portfolio assessments is to have students select samples from their own work to reflect on their development over time. Another is to give students criteria for performance to aim for and let them collaborate with teachers to develop goals (B) and standards for themselves. Another is to have students create their own rubrics—in small groups, as a whole class, or individually (C). Setting realistic, tangible goals for improvement, collaboratively with teachers (D), is another way of engaging active student participation.

64. B: Experts observe students are often defensive when their parents critique their writing, whereas when professionals emphasize the writing process over the end-product, students report they enjoy instructor feedback (A). When teachers treat writing as a process, this encourages students to explore all possibilities in a composition before choosing closure (B). If teachers divide writing into steps, students realize greater benefits, by understanding which specific aspect of their work teacher feedback is about (C), and by developing the ability to maintain more perspective about their work by viewing writing as a series of (recursive) steps, not an indivisible whole (D).

Copyright © Mometrix Media. You have been licensed one copy of this document for personal use only. Any other reproduction or redistribution is strictly prohibited. All rights reserved.
This content is provided for test preparation purposes only and does not imply an endorsement by Mometrix of any particular political, scientific, or religious point of view.

65. B: Having students write research questions, find sources, take notes, and make outlines (A) describes the step of independent student practice. Having students make outlines from their notes and classify information while providing them with support (B) describes the step of guided practices. Asking students how they found information and the students responding by describing all steps they took (C) relates to the step of a think check. Demonstrating identifying questions, how to find information, and categorize it (D) describes the step of teacher modeling.

66. D: Mastering academic language becomes increasingly complex as students begin incorporating it into their writing. As academic language is often formal and complex, young learners may struggle to use this type of language when engaging in writing activities. However, developing this skill is an essential component of building writing fluency, as it demonstrates a deeper understanding of the nuances of language. Educators can begin fostering students' ability to incorporate academic language by providing them with sentence frames to guide their writing. Sentence frames scaffold learning by serving as a structural and contextual framework for students to utilize when crafting sentences, thus prompting them to properly utilize academic language. This strategy promotes internalization of how to incorporate increasingly advanced vocabulary into writing, thus strengthening student understanding and promoting writing fluency development.

67. A: Audience members are most likely to retain the points of a speech or lecture if they are offered in the form of a story and the speaker uses language that is simple and direct enough to be transparent. The stories need to be simple, and must drive the speech directly toward an essential and clear point. Including anecdotes is most effective when the speaker uses storytelling techniques that will bring them alive, such as varying pace, pitch, and intensity, using body language to suggest a change in speakers, and using the stage to suggest a setting.

68. A: Experts do advise communications presenters to combine two or three types of media for the most effectiveness, rather than limiting themselves to only one (B). The presenter's budget will also necessarily influence their choice of media (C). For example, TV is more expensive than radio; radio is more expensive than paying a PR writer for print communications; and some presenters can produce their own news releases and photos at no additional cost. How long a communication is will affect the media choice (D), e.g., in terms of costs and of maintaining audience attention.

69. B: Although today digital text, images, and sound files can be reliably saved for longer periods of time, digital media are still not necessarily as permanent (a) or long lasting in the same form as text printed on paper, art painted on canvas, or music recorded in some other formats. However, digital media are more versatile (c): they can be displayed globally in multiple locations, on smartphones, palm devices, laptop screens, desktop monitors, giant public video screens, etc. They are more flexible (d): they can be sharpened, blurred, darkened, lightened; parts can be deleted, restored, duplicated, recombined, transposed, etc.; and changed/adapted for students with diverse needs. They can combine text, video, and audio, which print media cannot; enable students with learning challenges to select the most adaptive formats; and allow multimedia interactivity.

70. D: Credibility is related to how believable readers felt the author's writing was, which is a major element of whether the author's appeals changed the readers' minds. Clarity, another criterion for evaluating methods of appeal, is related to how clearly the author presented the content. Accuracy, an additional criterion, is related to whether the content that the author included was factually correct. Cohesion, also an evaluative criterion, has to do with how well the author's arguments and appeals are connected and related to one another, which helps readers understand them and holds their interest.

Copyright © Mometrix Media. You have been licensed one copy of this document for personal use only. Any other reproduction or redistribution is strictly prohibited. All rights reserved.
This content is provided for test preparation purposes only and does not imply an endorsement by Mometrix of any particular political, scientific, or religious point of view.

71. A: Considering audience is not necessary in order to determine purpose, so choice A is correct. Choice B is incorrect because writers should use audience and purpose to decide on the best structure and organization for those who will read the writing. Choice C is incorrect, as audience, along with purpose of writing, will determine what style and tone to use in a piece of writing, and will therefore affect word choice. Identifying an audience will also help in choosing specific words that will be most understandable and appealing to readers. Finally, choice D is incorrect because audience will also dictate how much time to spend on research. Some readers will expect more supporting evidence, while others will not.

72. A: The first step a reader should take in evaluating the arguments in an informational text is to identify the conclusion the author draws with the argument. The second step is to identify what premises or reasons support this conclusion. The third step is to clarify these premises or reasons by paraphrasing them in the reader's own words, which can also show whether the premises fit with the conclusion they should support. The reader can then list all premises in order, followed by the conclusion, and note any assumptions or premises necessary to support the conclusion that the author may have omitted. The next step is judging whether a deductive reasoning argument is valid, or whether an inductive reasoning argument uses true premises that support the conclusion.

73. D: Tracing and evaluating arguments and specific claims in a text are shared standards for grades 6 and 7, and delineating and evaluating arguments and specific claims in a text is a standard for grade 8 (a). Distinguishing whether claims are supported by evidence and reasons or not (b) is a part of the standard for grade 6 only. Assessing whether the reasoning in claims is sound and the evidence is relevant and sufficient to support the claims (c) is a part of the standards for grades 7 and 8. Recognizing whether irrelevant evidence has been introduced (d) is a part of the standard for grade 8 only.

74. C: Citing evidence of only one budget cut (A), even though it is the largest, is not sufficient evidence because it does not represent a significant proportion of all community colleges in the state. Similarly, citing only two examples (B), regardless of their prominence, does not represent a significant proportion of the total. Citing examples from 15 of 34 colleges (C) in the state shows that the general claim is true for a significant proportion of community colleges in the state. Citing specific cut amounts at all 34 colleges (D) is beyond sufficient, to the point of excess: reading/listening audiences would likely be so bored by this amount of evidence, it would distract them from accepting the claim.

Educating All Learners and Professional Practice

75. A: Rubrics are a type of evaluation tool that assign both overall scores and scores in individual component areas of an assignment. In each component area, the criteria used to assign scores for different levels of mastery are outlined. Therefore, students can see their overall grades on assignments, as well as how they performed in each component area. This helps students assess their strengths and weaknesses. Rubrics do not specifically track progress over time, though teachers could evaluate students using the same rubric at different points of the year and compare the results. Rubrics assess individual performance and do not compare students to their peers. Choice D describes a miscue analysis, which is a different type of assessment.

76. B: Reading curriculum designs may fail when one or more of their individual components fail (A); or when their components do not fail individually, but are incompatible with one another (C); or when personnel charged with implementing a design dislike or misunderstand it (D). Since there are multiple sources of failure, most curriculum designs are neither 100 percent failures nor 100

Copyright © Mometrix Media. You have been licensed one copy of this document for personal use only. Any other reproduction or redistribution is strictly prohibited. All rights reserved.
This content is provided for test preparation purposes only and does not imply an endorsement by Mometrix of any particular political, scientific, or religious point of view.

percent successes—informing the fact that an essential element of designing curriculum is to provide for continuous improvement (B), during and following the design process.

77. B: Schemata are units of existing knowledge used to make sense of newly encountered information. Readers rely on their existing schemata to make sense of information encountered in new texts. Therefore, activating prior knowledge is a key component of schema theory. For example, a child may know that flowers require water to grow. He may use this existing schema to make sense of a new text about the desert, which indicates that few plants grow there. Summarizing, identifying main idea, and recognizing story elements all require finding key information within a text, but they do not necessarily relate this information to what was already known about the topic prior to reading.

78. D: If the student is having difficulties with comprehension rather than decoding, he will likely benefit from having the information represented in multiple ways. Seeing visual representations of the words and content may assist him with comprehension. Additionally, multimedia textbooks often contain features like hyperlinked vocabulary words that display definitions when clicked. Choices A and B would only read the same vocabulary words aloud without any additional explanation or visuals to assist with comprehension. An outline also presents the information in text rather than focusing on visual clues.

79. D: Sending home leveled texts ensures that families have access to books in students' instructional reading levels. Providing the books allows students to read immediately and free of charge without requiring any trips to a library or bookstore. Choice A is also helpful, but without providing appropriate books, there is no guarantee that students will have access to reading materials. Notifying parents of which phonics skills the class practiced can also be helpful, but without providing additional information or materials, parents may not know how to best help their children practice these skills. Studying spelling words addresses the words in isolation rather than providing opportunities to read in context and practice decoding, comprehension, and fluency.

80. A: Not all world cultures have spoken languages (B); e.g., deaf cultures sign but do not speak. Not all cultures have written languages (C); e.g., some island and tribal cultures have exclusively oral traditions, with no formal system of written symbols. All world cultures use social conventions and body language (D)—though the meanings of gestures vary across cultures more than facial expressions, all cultures use them—AND all cultures use some kind of language, whether it is spoken, written, signed (A), or any combination of these.

81. D: Teachers can much more easily diagnose specific reading difficulties in a few students at a time within a small group than in a whole class. Small-group instruction also makes it easier to design interventions for several students on similar reading levels with similar problem areas within a small group than for all students in a large class.

82. B: A teacher should use guided reading lessons, not skills-focused lessons, to monitor how well students are applying the skills they have learned to reading text (A). Guided reading lessons are not the best format for helping students master comprehension strategies (B), phonics knowledge, phonemic decoding strategies, key vocabulary, or other fundamental reading skills if students have basic knowledge gaps in these. Skills-focused lessons are more effective to develop these skills before students can apply them to read for and discuss text meanings (C) with teacher support (D).

83. B: Although concurrent learning disabilities and disorders are common, e.g., attentional, receptive, and expressive language difficulties often coexist, an expressive language disorder (A) would have the most direct impact on a student's speaking and writing performance and

Copyright © Mometrix Media. You have been licensed one copy of this document for personal use only. Any other reproduction or redistribution is strictly prohibited. All rights reserved.
This content is provided for test preparation purposes only and does not imply an endorsement by Mometrix of any particular political, scientific, or religious point of view.

instruction. A receptive language disorder (B) would have the most direct impact on a student's listening and reading skills. An articulation disorder (C) would have the most direct impact on a student's correct or intelligible speech production or pronunciation. A movement disorder (D) could have impacts on speech production, but by itself it should not affect language or reading development.

84. D: Testing instrument reliability is indicated if the test yields consistent results across repeated administrations. Measuring the specific skill that it claims to measure (A) indicates test validity, not reliability. Tests with clearly written items are typically more reliable than those using open-ended, ambiguous questions (B). Tests that measure a skill using a fairly large quantity of items are typically more reliable than tests using only a few, very focused items (C).

85. A: From a literature review, researchers (c. Henderson and Mapp, 2002) concluded that students whose families are involved in their learning get higher grades, take more advanced classes, have higher graduation rates, and are more likely to attend postsecondary education. Students perform best academically when their parents adopt varied roles in their learning, like not only participating in school events and activities, but also helping at home, contributing to key school program decisions, guiding children through the system, etc. (B). Students with involved families also attend school more regularly, have more positive attitudes toward school, and demonstrate better behavior in school (C). Finally, students from diverse backgrounds perform better academically from school-family collaboration to bridge cultural gaps (D).

86. C: Conflict is often viewed as negative, but this view is neither necessary nor accurate (A); conflict is natural in human interactions and can be viewed as an opportunity for social reform and moral growth (C). Conflict cannot be avoided (A), as it is ubiquitous in everyday life as well as educational decisions. Experts observe that understanding oneself is an essential basis for resolving conflict (B) through negotiation and cooperation. While conflict commonly occurs, it has been described more often than analyzed, not vice versa (D).

87. B: Graphic organizers help students understand concepts by presenting abstract ideas in visual form (A), making them easier to comprehend through pictures or images than through words or numbers. They also enable students to classify or categorize concepts (D) by comparing, contrasting, separating, and grouping them (C).

88. A: Researchers identify norm-referenced tests, including norm-referenced reading tests, as better for assessing abstract cognitive levels and criterion-referenced tests as better for assessing concrete cognitive levels. They also identify norm-referenced tests as better for assessing heterogeneous groups and criterion-referenced as better for homogeneous groups (B). Also, norm-referenced tests are better for assessing wider ranges of ability and criterion-referenced for narrower ability ranges (C). Finally, they identify norm-referenced tests as better for assessing wider ranges of outcomes and objectives and criterion-referenced for narrower ranges of these (D).

89. A: The NEA recommends effective school-family-community partnership strategies, including taking time to build one-to-one, learning-related family-educator relationships and discuss and agree on how best to collaborate for student success. Another is setting, communicating, and supporting high, rigorous expectations, particularly for at-risk and marginal students (B), and giving them needed support for succeeding. Another is providing support for faculty and other professionals to overcome cultural, linguistic, and class barriers, rather than just requiring that they do so (C). Establishing student-community connections not only gives students relevant, hands-on learning, but also demonstrates student and school community service (D).

Copyright © Mometrix Media. You have been licensed one copy of this document for personal use only. Any other reproduction or redistribution is strictly prohibited. All rights reserved.
This content is provided for test preparation purposes only and does not imply an endorsement by Mometrix of any particular political, scientific, or religious point of view.

90. D: Reader's theaters are literacy activities in which students assume the roles and act out the dialogue of characters from familiar plays or stories with the intention of developing prosodic reading and ultimately, reading fluency skills. During these activities, students are encouraged to focus on expression, intonation, pace, and volume to reflect that of spoken language. Effective implementation of reader's theaters in the elementary classroom requires the teacher to be cognizant of varying reading fluency levels and to differentiate the activity accordingly. In the given scenario, the teacher differentiates the activity by grouping students based on ability and providing scripts aligned with their reading fluency skills. To further modify this activity, the teacher could incorporate guided reading sessions with each group to support struggling readers in mastering their lines and improving overall comprehension and fluency. Doing so would promote students' confidence and engagement in reading while providing the necessary support to ensure all students build upon their reading fluency skills.

Copyright © Mometrix Media. You have been licensed one copy of this document for personal use only. Any other reproduction or redistribution is strictly prohibited. All rights reserved.
This content is provided for test preparation purposes only and does not imply an endorsement by Mometrix of any particular political, scientific, or religious point of view.

Practice Test #2

Foundations of Reading

1. A teacher wants to determine a student's accuracy and reading rate in order to determine if a text is in the student's frustration, instructional, or independent reading level. Which of the following assessments should she use?

a. Authentic assessment task
b. Rubric
c. Guided reading observation
d. Running record

2. During a small-group activity, a teacher asks her students to repeat a CVC word slowly, stretching out the sounds. As students repeat the word, they slide one penny forward for each sound they hear. Which phonemic awareness skill are students practicing?

a. Blending
b. Segmenting
c. Phoneme identification
d. Phoneme isolation

3. Which statement best describes the relationship between reading and writing?

a. Reading is a prerequisite skill that should be taught before writing.
b. Writing is a prerequisite skill that should be taught before reading.
c. Reading and writing are interrelated and should be taught together.
d. The order of instruction does not matter, but one should be taught first to avoid cognitive overload.

4. What is true about pre-production activities that teachers can use to encourage English-language speech by ELL students?

a. Narrating students' actions will simply make them self-conscious.
b. The activities that teachers use should involve hands-on learning.
c. It is more important that activities use speech than have meaning.
d. Language functions are irrelevant if students complete the lesson.

5. A teacher is introducing a new phonics skill to her students. She begins with explicit instruction on the skill, followed by modeling. Which instructional component should come next?

a. Independent practice
b. Guided practice
c. Generalization
d. Feedback

6. Which of the following words contains a consonant digraph?

a. Swim
b. Blue
c. From
d. Cheek

Copyright © Mometrix Media. You have been licensed one copy of this document for personal use only. Any other reproduction or redistribution is strictly prohibited. All rights reserved.
This content is provided for test preparation purposes only and does not imply an endorsement by Mometrix of any particular political, scientific, or religious point of view.

7. Which of the following options best describes decodable texts?

a. They contain a predictable text structure that allows emergent readers to guess what will come next.
b. They allow students to apply newly learned phonics skills while reading new texts.
c. They contain a large amount of content-related words to reinforce vocabulary development.
d. They are books with complex plot development that are ideal for close reading analysis.

8. A student participating in a reading assessment uses information from illustrations in the text he or she is reading to support reading performance. The student is using which kind of cue?

a. A visual cue
b. A meaning cue
c. A structural cue
d. A graphophonic cue

9. What is orthographic processing?

a. The ability to separate spoken words into component sounds
b. Understanding the predictable sound each letter makes
c. Recognizing letter patterns that make up words or word parts
d. Understanding spoken words

10. Regarding the relationship of phonemic awareness to reading and writing, which is NOT true?

a. Phonemic awareness is a listening and speaking skill, not a reading and writing skill.
b. Including print letters and words in teaching phonemic awareness is more effective.
c. Using print letters and words alone in teaching phonemic awareness is sufficient.
d. Pointing to printed letters while saying them aloud to draw attention to sound-letter connections is helpful.

11. A teacher asks her students to say /ake/. She then tells students to add different consonant sounds to the beginning of /ake/ to see which real and nonsense words they can form. Which component of phonological awareness are students practicing in this activity?

a. Syllabification
b. Onsets and rimes
c. Phoneme isolation
d. Segmentation

12. In phonics instruction, what is accurate relative to phonological discrimination exercises?

a. Children's invented spellings may omit consonants, but never vowels.
b. Children can discriminate short vowels more easily than long vowels.
c. Children can discriminate long vowels more easily than short vowels.
d. Children must learn to discriminate short vowels before long vowels in words.

Copyright © Mometrix Media. You have been licensed one copy of this document for personal use only. Any other reproduction or redistribution is strictly prohibited. All rights reserved.
This content is provided for test preparation purposes only and does not imply an endorsement by Mometrix of any particular political, scientific, or religious point of view.

13. The most effective strategy for decoding irregular sight words is:

a. Segmenting sight words into syllables. Beginning readers are understandably nervous when encountering a long word that isn't familiar. Blocking off all but a single syllable at a time renders a word manageable and allows the reader a sense of control over the act of reading.
b. Word families. By grouping the sight word with similar words, patterns emerge.
c. A phonemic approach. When students understand the connection between individual words and their sounds, they will be able to sound out any sight word they encounter.
d. None; irregular sight words cannot be decoded. Readers must learn to recognize these as whole words on sight.

14. "Decoding" is also called:

a. Remediation
b. Deciphering
c. Alphabetic principle
d. Deconstruction

15. While reading an expository text aloud to students, a teacher makes the following comments.

> "'The cheetah can accelerate to its top speed in about three seconds.' Hmm, I'm not sure what accelerate means. Let me read that again to see if the sentence has any clues. 'The cheetah can accelerate to its top speed in about three seconds.' It has something to do with the cheetah getting faster, so I think accelerate means to speed up."

What is the teacher demonstrating in this activity?

a. Forming mental images
b. Making a prediction
c. Thinking aloud
d. Visualizing

16. "Code knowledge" facilitates reading fluency because:

a. It brings the entirety of the student's previous experience to bear on decoding a text.
b. It offers a framework for organizing new information by assigning code words to sets of ideas.
c. There is no such thing as "code knowledge." The correct term is "core knowledge."
d. It offers a systematic approach to untangling the wide variety of vowel sounds when an unfamiliar word is encountered.

17. When assessing error patterns in a student's reading, which is most detrimental to reading proficiency?

a. Substitution of "control" for "contrariness"
b. Substitution of "resistant" for "recalcitrant"
c. Substituting a noun, not a verb, for a noun
d. Substituting for errors informed by context

18. What is a morpheme?

a. The smallest unit of language with meaning
b. The smallest unit of speech
c. A letter or group of letters representing a single sound
d. A unit of spoken language in a word, which contains a single vowel sound

Copyright © Mometrix Media. You have been licensed one copy of this document for personal use only. Any other reproduction or redistribution is strictly prohibited. All rights reserved.
This content is provided for test preparation purposes only and does not imply an endorsement by Mometrix of any particular political, scientific, or religious point of view.

19. In which of the following examples does the root word change when the suffix -*ment* is added?

a. Treat
b. Replace
c. Establish
d. Argue

20. Which of the following statements is true regarding word walls?

a. They should mainly focus on content-related words.
b. They should contain only words that are difficult for students to spell independently.
c. They should be flexible, allowing words to be added and removed throughout the year.
d. They are only needed for students in the emergent stage of reading development.

21. To teach students nonverbal communication skills, what have some teachers discovered through experience?

a. Nonverbal communication should be taught to students in large portions.
b. Nonverbal communication should be taught using appropriate situations.
c. Nonverbal communication does not require students to have confidence.
d. Nonverbal communication does not involve creativity from the students.

22. A student incorrectly pronounces the word *rattle* with a long vowel *a*. The teacher explains a general rule to the student about splitting doubled consonants. This instructional strategy focuses most on using which of these?

a. Structural analysis
b. Spelling patterns
c. Syllabication
d. Morphemes

23. In investigating the best instructional strategies and tools for planning and implementing school reading programs, what have researchers found?

a. Explicit phonics instruction enables higher achievement only for at-risk students.
b. Instruction incorporating decodable books has been discredited by researchers.
c. Student use of word identification strategies is unrelated to what text they read.
d. Prior student literacy knowledge helps to develop sound-spelling understanding.

24. According to experts, which of the following is an accurate distinction regarding phonological awareness and phonemic awareness?

a. Phonological awareness distinguishes speech sounds from meanings.
b. There is no real distinction; they are synonyms used interchangeably.
c. Phonological awareness involves sounds, phonemic involves speech.
d. Phonemic awareness is the less sophisticated level between the two.

25. Government-funded research has found which of the following about phonics instruction?

a. It is equally effective regardless of whether it is systematic and explicit or not.
b. It is more effective for children of certain socioeconomic levels than for others.
c. It is equally effective regardless of the age or grade levels when introduced.
d. It is more effective when students can understand and apply their learning.

Copyright © Mometrix Media. You have been licensed one copy of this document for personal use only. Any other reproduction or redistribution is strictly prohibited. All rights reserved.
This content is provided for test preparation purposes only and does not imply an endorsement by Mometrix of any particular political, scientific, or religious point of view.

26. Which of these is one of the signs that a student has difficulty with retaining reading?

a. The student's oral reading disregards punctuation.
b. The student's reading omits, or disregards, details.
c. The student's insertion of additional words that are not in the text is frequent.
d. The student's connection of text ideas is deficient.

27. A fourth-grade teacher has students individually read aloud from the following passage:

During the confusion and bewilderment of the second day Mary hid herself in the nursery and was forgotten by everyone. Nobody thought of her, nobody wanted her, and strange things happened of which she knew nothing. Mary alternately cried and slept through the hours. She only knew that people were ill and that she heard mysterious and frightening sounds. Once she crept into the dining-room and found it empty, though a partly finished meal was on the table and chairs and plates looked as if they had been hastily pushed back when the diners rose suddenly for some reason.

Burnett, Frances H. *The Secret Garden*. The Phillips Publishing Company, 1911.

As each student reads aloud, the teacher records students' progress. Below is an example of data collected from one student's reading of the passage:

Total Words in Passage: 100
Time allotted: One minute
Total Words Read: 100
Errors: 11
Words Correct Per Minute (WCPM): 89

Based on the information above, the teacher is most likely assessing which of the following skills related to reading fluency?

a. Prosody
b. Decoding skills
c. Orthographic processing
d. Automaticity

Refer to the following for question 28:

Prior to beginning a social studies unit focused on the United States Constitution, a fourth-grade teacher implements an introductory activity that includes several vocabulary words related to the unit, their definitions, and examples of their usage in sentences.

28. Which of the following additional strategies could the teacher implement to further strengthen students' understanding of academic language?

a. Assign a project in which students write their own version of a constitution
b. Conduct sentence dictation exercises using new vocabulary from the unit
c. Have students create their own flash cards based on the new vocabulary from the unit
d. Assign an expository essay assignment in which students write about the development of the United States Constitution

Copyright © Mometrix Media. You have been licensed one copy of this document for personal use only. Any other reproduction or redistribution is strictly prohibited. All rights reserved.
This content is provided for test preparation purposes only and does not imply an endorsement by Mometrix of any particular political, scientific, or religious point of view.

29. Guiding students in locating clue words within a text to determine the meaning of unfamiliar vocabulary is an example of a strategy aimed at developing which of the following skills related to reading comprehension and fluency?

a. Structural analysis
b. Critical analysis
c. Contextual analysis
d. Automaticity

Text Comprehension and Analysis

30. Based on assessment data, a teacher identifies a small group of students who would benefit from targeted instruction on using textual evidence to support their answers. Which strategy would be most helpful for the teacher to model to assist students with this type of test question?

a. Underlining passages in the text where answers are located
b. Reading the passage once to identify the main idea, and then rereading to look for details
c. Reading each answer choice carefully before selecting an answer, crossing out answers as they are eliminated
d. Completing a story map while reading the story

31. Which instructional strategy would be most appropriate to assist a student with retention difficulties in analyzing the plot of a fictional text?

a. Providing the student with a story map
b. Having the student read the story twice before responding to questions
c. Playing an audio version of the story rather than having the student read a printed version
d. Asking the student to complete a KWL chart before and after reading

32. Which of the following sentences would best help model the concept of figurative language?

a. The sky was dark and gray, warning that a storm was approaching.
b. The snow was a wet blanket covering the earth.
c. Taking care of a puppy requires time and patience.
d. The cold, wet raindrops splashed on my glasses and made it difficult to see.

33. Before asking students to read a new fiction book independently, the teacher conducts a picture walk with the class. What is the teacher's primary goal for conducting the picture walk?

a. Encouraging the use of syntactic cues
b. Setting a purpose for reading
c. Activating students' prior knowledge
d. Developing students' metacognitive skills

34. Cause and effect, compare and contrast, and time order are all examples of what?

a. Literary devices
b. Literary elements
c. Genres
d. Text structures

Copyright © Mometrix Media. You have been licensed one copy of this document for personal use only. Any other reproduction or redistribution is strictly prohibited. All rights reserved.
This content is provided for test preparation purposes only and does not imply an endorsement by Mometrix of any particular political, scientific, or religious point of view.

35. Reciprocal teaching activities focus on four main reading strategies. What is the fourth strategy, in addition to summarizing, questioning, and predicting?

a. Evaluating
b. Connecting
c. Retelling
d. Clarifying

36. A fifth-grade teacher introduces the skill of underlining text evidence to answer comprehension questions. He then models how to use this strategy using a sample text and related questions. Next, the class uses the strategy together to answer a new set of questions, with the teacher providing feedback on each attempt. Which activity would be the best choice to come next?

a. Give students a passage and questions to complete independently using the underlining strategy.
b. Reteach how to use the underlining strategy using different examples.
c. Ask students to use this strategy when they take tests in the future.
d. Test students on their ability to use the underlining strategy to answer comprehension questions.

37. Fourth-grade students in Mr. Lee's class are writing persuasive speeches on topics of their choice and presenting them to the class. One student, Caleb, gives a speech regarding the types of foods the school cafeteria should serve. He states, "The cafeteria should stop serving meatloaf because nobody likes it." After the speech, Mr. Lee asks Caleb what research he conducted to arrive at that conclusion. Caleb responds by saying, "Nobody at my lunch table ever eats it. They just end up throwing it away at the end of lunch." Which type of faulty reasoning should Mr. Lee address with Caleb?

a. Illogical conclusion
b. Overgeneralization
c. Personal bias
d. Circular reasoning

38. Joseph is reading a book with fictional characters who live in modern times but travel back to the American Revolution to fight with the colonial soldiers. This book contains elements of which two genres of fiction?

a. Folktales and realistic fiction
b. Fantasy and historical fiction
c. Fable and fantasy
d. Historical fiction and folktale

39. Which of the following questions is focused on students' aesthetic responses to a text?

a. Which character is the protagonist in the story?
b. What is the conflict in the story?
c. How did you feel when the character was being treated poorly by her friends?
d. What genre does this story fit into?

Copyright © Mometrix Media. You have been licensed one copy of this document for personal use only. Any other reproduction or redistribution is strictly prohibited. All rights reserved.
This content is provided for test preparation purposes only and does not imply an endorsement by Mometrix of any particular political, scientific, or religious point of view.

40. A teacher gives students an unfamiliar text. Without doing a picture walk or pre-teaching any vocabulary words, she asks them to read it once independently. During this first reading, students are told to identify the overall meaning of the text, as well as note their initial impressions. Students discuss these responses with their peers. The teacher then asks the students to read a specific portion of the text a second time, analyzing the author's use of figurative language. Students then discuss their thoughts again. The teacher then asks the students to reread the text a third time, comparing and contrasting the main character with the main character in another text they have read. Students once again share their responses with peers. Which type of reading activity does this example demonstrate?

a. Guided reading
b. SQ3R
c. Close reading
d. Scanning

41. Using E. B. White's *Stuart Little* as an example, which response represents evaluative comprehension?

a. "Stuart Little, who is the main character in this story, is a mouse."
b. "Stuart's parents, Mr. and Mrs. Frederick C. Little, are humans."
c. "Stuart's size and doing things a mouse can do help his family."
d. "Stuart likes to be first up in the morning; I like to sleep late."

42. Which of the following questions requires students to make an inference about a fictional text?

a. Did the author support her points with strong evidence?
b. How do you think the character felt when she said that?
c. What do you think will happen next?
d. Does this character remind you of any characters in other books you have read?

43. Which of the following instructional strategies helps students ask questions about text, make predictions, and then read further to confirm or deny what they predicted?

a. Gist
b. DRTA
c. Fishbowl
d. Cornell Notes

Refer to the following for question 44:

A teacher has given the first paragraph of an essay to her students to analyze and discuss.

> Americans have struggled with cigarettes far too long. Until now, it has been a personal choice to smoke (or not), but the time for change is rapidly approaching. Local legislation has already begun for schools, restaurants, arenas, and other public places to be smoke-free. Years ago, cigarette smoking was presented by the media as being fashionable, even sexy. In magazines, movies, and later in television, celebrities would indulge themselves with a smoke and even be paid to endorse a brand. As recently as 1975, it was common for talk show hosts like Tom Snyder and Johnny Carson to keep a cigarette burning. Cigarette smoking in America has persisted in spite of frightening concerns like lung cancer and emphysema. Over the years, the tobacco industry has sought to diffuse strong evidence that smoking is harmful. However, the myth of "safe cigarettes," questions about nicotine addiction, and

Copyright © Mometrix Media. You have been licensed one copy of this document for personal use only. Any other reproduction or redistribution is strictly prohibited. All rights reserved.
This content is provided for test preparation purposes only and does not imply an endorsement by Mometrix of any particular political, scientific, or religious point of view.

denials about the dangers of secondhand smoke have proven to be propaganda and lies.

44. This is a(n) ____________ essay:

a. compare/contrast
b. persuasive
c. narrative
d. analytic

45. A teacher gives students a story map to complete while reading a realistic fiction text. They are asked to record the characters, setting, problem, events, and solution. Which level of comprehension does this activity address?

a. Affective
b. Literal
c. Inferential
d. Evaluative

46. Experts (Wallace et al., 2007) recommend instructional writing strategies for improving reading comprehension. Which one of these does this through helping students to see information from various perspectives?

a. Read, respond, revisit, discuss
b. Four square graphic organizer
c. About/point
d. Cubing

47. The use of which graphic organizer best supports schema theory?

a. Problem-solution chart
b. Think-pair-share chart
c. Sequence chain
d. KWL chart

48. Students read a text wherein the author presents a point; provides evidence to support it; appeals to reader emotion, logic, or belief in author credibility; and raises and refutes a counterpoint. Based on this description, the students can identify author purpose as which of these?

a. To inform the audience
b. To entertain the reader
c. To persuade the reader
d. To analyze the subject

Copyright © Mometrix Media. You have been licensed one copy of this document for personal use only. Any other reproduction or redistribution is strictly prohibited. All rights reserved.
This content is provided for test preparation purposes only and does not imply an endorsement by Mometrix of any particular political, scientific, or religious point of view.

49. A fifth-grade teacher assigns students to independently read a passage from a work of fictional literature and complete various annotations as they do so. Below is an example of one student's work.

> **Directions**: As you read, highlight any unfamiliar vocabulary words. Underline any key details or information. Add questions throughout the text as you go along.
>
> "Before I was two years old a circumstance happened which I have never forgotten. It was early in the spring; there had been a little frost in the night, and a light mist still hung over the woods and meadows. I and the other colts were feeding at the lower part of the field when we heard, quite in the distance, what sounded like the cry of dogs. The oldest of the colts raised his head, pricked his ears, and said, "There are the hounds!" and immediately cantered off, followed by the rest of us to the upper part of the field, where we could look over the hedge and see several fields beyond.
>
> (Were they afraid of the dogs?)
>
> My mother and an old riding horse of our master's were also standing near, and seemed to know all about it. (What did they know about?)
>
> "They have found a hare." said my mother, "and if they come this way we shall see the hunt."
>
> And soon the dogs were all tearing down the field of young wheat next to ours. I never heard such a noise as they made. They did not bark, nor howl, nor whine, but kept on a "yo! Yo, o, o! Yo! Yo, o, o!" at the top of their voices. After them came a number of men on horseback, some of them in green coats, all galloping as fast as they could. (Where did the men come from? What were they going to do?)
>
> The old horse snorted and looked eagerly after them, and we young colts wanted to be galloping with them, but they were soon away into the fields lower down; here it seemed as if they had come to a stand; the dogs left off barking, and ran about every way with their noses to the ground.
>
> Sewell, Anna. *Black Beauty*. Jarrold & Sons, 1877. Pp. 12-13

Based on the information in the example above, the teacher is most likely implementing which of the following instructional strategies to promote reading comprehension and critical analysis skills?

a. Guided reading
b. Close reading
c. Chunking
d. Read-pair-share

Copyright © Mometrix Media. You have been licensed one copy of this document for personal use only. Any other reproduction or redistribution is strictly prohibited. All rights reserved.
This content is provided for test preparation purposes only and does not imply an endorsement by Mometrix of any particular political, scientific, or religious point of view.

50. A fourth-grade teacher is preparing a lesson in which students will read an informational text about agricultural practices. During the lesson, the teacher aims to promote comprehension and analysis by calling upon students' prior knowledge and promoting active engagement with the text. Which of the following pre-reading strategies would be most effective in achieving this goal?

a. Leading a whole-class discussion about agricultural methods used throughout different regions
b. Having students complete a KWL chart about agricultural practices
c. Providing direct instruction on key information related to the text
d. Assigning students to complete a Venn diagram to compare and contrast ancient and modern agricultural practices

Refer to the following for question 51:

A sixth-grade teacher is preparing a science lesson in which students will read from the following passage:

> Rocks are all around us, from our backyards and playgrounds to mountaintops and even the ocean floor. Rocks are an important part of forming landscapes, supporting ecosystems, and providing resources for many human activities. Rocks can be categorized as igneous, sedimentary, or metamorphic, and each can be recognized by its distinct features.
>
> Igneous rocks are created when lava cools off and becomes solid. When this occurs underground, it forms intrusive igneous rocks. Lava that reaches the Earth's surface, such as after a volcanic eruption, cools quickly and forms extrusive igneous rocks. These rocks usually have a glass-like appearance and can contain minerals such as quartz, feldspar, and biotite.
>
> Sedimentary rocks form from sediments, which include pieces of other rocks and the remains of plants and animals. Over a very long period of time, these sediments compress together to form sedimentary rocks, such as limestone, sandstone, and shale. You can often find fossils and layers in these rocks that can tell us a lot about Earth's history.
>
> Metamorphic rocks are created when rocks are exposed to high heat and pressure within the Earth's crust. This causes the rocks to go through physical and chemical changes that form them into metamorphic rocks. Some examples include marble, slate, and quartzite. Metamorphic rocks typically appear layered and can contain minerals such as garnet, kyanite, and corundum.
>
> Knowing the characteristics of different kinds of rocks and how they are formed helps us learn about the Earth's history. Each type of rock provides valuable information about how our planet was shaped over many millions of years.

Copyright © Mometrix Media. You have been licensed one copy of this document for personal use only. Any other reproduction or redistribution is strictly prohibited. All rights reserved.
This content is provided for test preparation purposes only and does not imply an endorsement by Mometrix of any particular political, scientific, or religious point of view.

51. Considering the nature of the passage above, which of the following styles of graphic organizer would be most effective for promoting students' reading comprehension?

a. A Venn diagram
b. A KWL chart
c. A timeline
d. An outline

52. A fifth-grade teacher is working to build students' evaluative reading comprehension skills. The teacher plans to have students read an informational text, and then respond to a series of prompts in their reader's response journals. Which of the following questions would be most suitable for developing students' ability to read evaluatively?

a. "Do you agree or disagree with the author's point of view? Why?"
b. "How did the author's language impact the overall tone of the text?"
c. "What is one new thing you learned from reading the text? What is one thing you still do not understand?"
d. "Identify the central idea of the text. What are some key details that support the central idea?"

Oral and Written Communication

53. Aidan, a fifth-grade student, writes a letter to the cafeteria manager at his school asking her to implement a schoolwide composting program. He outlines reasons why the composting program would benefit the environment and save the school money on waste disposal costs. He ends his letter by politely asking her to consider the proposal. What is Aidan's primary purpose for writing?

a. To inform
b. To persuade
c. To entertain
d. To describe

54. Which statement is correct about how teachers can model appropriate listening and speaking behaviors for students?

a. Teachers can model these when they facilitate book discussions, not in everyday conversations.
b. Teachers can model these better when giving whole-class instruction rather than small-group teaching.
c. Teachers can model these more authentically in one-to-one conversations than in discussions of media.
d. Teachers can model these and support them by thinking aloud about specific content they teach.

55. Which of the following best describes Chomsky's theory of Universal Grammar?

a. All languages have a level of structure in common.
b. All languages have a similar order of acquisition.
c. All languages can be acquired in the same amount of time.
d. All languages have equivalent rules, though ordering may be different.

Copyright © Mometrix Media. You have been licensed one copy of this document for personal use only. Any other reproduction or redistribution is strictly prohibited. All rights reserved.
This content is provided for test preparation purposes only and does not imply an endorsement by Mometrix of any particular political, scientific, or religious point of view.

56. Students in Ms. Dean's class discuss their existing knowledge and thoughts about sustainable farming practices before conducting any research on the topic. Next, they research the topic, locating four reputable print sources and conducting one interview with an expert in the field. They take notes, recording key information from each source. They use their notes from all of the sources to write a research report on the topic. They also complete a written reflection outlining how their initial thoughts have changed as a result of the new information gathered from the sources. Which comprehension strategy are students demonstrating?

a. Evaluating
b. Inferring
c. Drawing conclusions
d. Synthesizing

57. When teachers assign students to take research notes on sources they find and read, what do they also need to advise students to do?

a. To make more generalized notes rather than more detailed notes
b. To note both quotations and paraphrases without differentiating
c. To differentiate quoting, paraphrasing, and commentaries clearly
d. To note both their own paraphrases and commentaries the same

58. While speaking to his friend, a fifth-grade student says, "Hey, you should read this book. It's awesome." Later, while presenting an oral book report in front of his class and teacher, he says, "This book is full of suspense. The author leaves you wondering if the main character will be rescued from the mountain before it is too late. I highly recommend you read it to find out if he is rescued in time." This example best demonstrates the role of what in language usage?

a. Social context
b. Cultural context
c. Contextual clues
d. Personal context

Refer to the following for question 59:

A seventh-grade teacher asks the reading teacher to suggest a lesson that students will find simultaneously challenging and fun. The reading teacher suggests the class read fairy tales from both Hans Christian Anderson and the Brothers Grimm and have a rapid-paced, energetic discussion about the many similarities and differences between the two while the teacher lists them on the board.

59. The individual strategies the students will employ are:

a. Collaborative learning and genre
b. Brainstorming and a compare/contrast strategy
c. Collaborative learning and brainstorming
d. Analyzing and genre

Refer to the following for question 60:

> A class will visit an assisted living facility to interview residents about their lives. Each group of three has selected a theme such as love, work, or personal accomplishment and written several questions around that theme. Next each group practices

Copyright © Mometrix Media. You have been licensed one copy of this document for personal use only. Any other reproduction or redistribution is strictly prohibited. All rights reserved.
This content is provided for test preparation purposes only and does not imply an endorsement by Mometrix of any particular political, scientific, or religious point of view.

interviewing one another. The teacher then asks all the students to discuss the questions that caused them to respond most thoughtfully, as well as those they were less inspired by. The students decided the questions that were easiest to respond to were those that asked for very specific information; for example, one inspiring question was, "Please tell me about something you learned to do as a child that affected the direction of your life." Those that were uninspiring were too broad, for example, "Please tell me about your happiest memory."

60. The teacher wants the students to apply what they've learned across content areas. Which of the following strategies would be most effective?

a. Students will interview a family member, asking the same questions.
b. Students will write a personal piece in which they address the same questions.
c. Students will do online research about the cultural, economic, or political events that were occurring during the specific time about which they've written.
d. Students pretend to be the interviewee and rewrite the piece from a first-person point of view.

Refer to the following for question 61:

A reading teacher is working with a student who has just moved to Texas from Korea. The child knows very few words in English. The teacher offers her a picture book of Korean folk tales. Using words and gestures, the teacher asks her to "read" one folk tale. The child "reads" the familiar tale in Korean. The teacher then writes key English words on the board and asks the child to find those words in the book. When the child finds the words, they read them together.

61. By using this strategy, the teacher is taking care to consider what type of load?

a. Language load
b. Cognitive load
c. Bilingual load
d. Cultural load

62. What is an example of the phonemic awareness instructional strategy of keyword substitution?

a. "Show, show, show your shoat, shently..."
b. "How much is that window in the doggie"
c. "'Twas brillig, and the slithy toves / Did..."
d. "Owe, owe, owe our oat, ently own the..."

63. Regarding instruction in speaking and listening, which of these have researchers found about the relationship between the time people spend using these skills and the time schools spend developing them?

a. Schools spend more time developing these skills than people spend using them.
b. Schools spend about the same amount of time on these skills as people use them.
c. Schools spend an opposite amount of time that people use these skills on developing them.
d. Schools spend only slightly less time on teaching these skills than people spend to use them.

Copyright © Mometrix Media. You have been licensed one copy of this document for personal use only. Any other reproduction or redistribution is strictly prohibited. All rights reserved.
This content is provided for test preparation purposes only and does not imply an endorsement by Mometrix of any particular political, scientific, or religious point of view.

64. Among principles of effective writing instruction, which of these reflects teaching discourse knowledge that enables more effective student writing?

a. Varying levels of explicit instruction, using small groups, and varying amounts of writing instruction time
b. Allowing sufficient time for systematic writing opportunities in both ELA classes and all content subjects
c. Incorporating reasons and methods for explicit writing instruction, including feedback and collaboration
d. Organizing writing effectively for various subjects, plus spelling, vocabulary, syntax, etc., for the subjects

65. A teacher who has integrated student smartphone use into the curriculum for doing research and completing assignments recommends a virtual field trip as an introductory activity for educators wanting to follow suit. What can teachers and students do during this activity?

a. Teachers can have students find more information by visiting a website, not a computer lab.
b. Teachers can locate experts in pertinent fields, but they will not speak directly with students.
c. Teachers can record the calls, but students cannot hear both ends of a teacher conversation.
d. Teachers can have students ask their own questions to direct the ending of the conversation.

66. Which of the following statements applies to presenting information clearly in a written speech?

a. A speechwriter need not define the purpose of a speech beforehand.
b. Logical organization may be sacrificed to prioritize audience engagement.
c. Making an outline of a speech causes a rigid structure and may make a speech boring.
d. Grammar and word choice should reflect natural spoken language.

67. Which type of nonverbal message deals with belonging, control, respect, or disapproval?

a. Emotive messages
b. Relational messages
c. Relationship messages
d. Interpersonal messages

68. What is an accurate reflection of criteria for clear, concise speech presentations?

a. A speaker should not take three or more minutes more to get to the point.
b. A speaker should not pause before answering audience questions.
c. A speaker should include as many anecdotes and details as possible.
d. A speaker should include both necessary and interesting information.

69. Which of the following statements is correct regarding effective speech delivery?

a. Speakers should avoid practicing speeches to appear spontaneous.
b. Verbal and nonverbal communication should seem equally natural.
c. Speakers should avoid using humor because it will distract the audience.
d. Random movements can help sustain the attention of the audience.

Copyright © Mometrix Media. You have been licensed one copy of this document for personal use only. Any other reproduction or redistribution is strictly prohibited. All rights reserved.
This content is provided for test preparation purposes only and does not imply an endorsement by Mometrix of any particular political, scientific, or religious point of view.

70. Which of the following best demonstrates writing appropriately for a specific task, purpose, and audience?

a. Using jargon in a book report that will be read aloud to classmates
b. Using simple language when describing a new procedure to expert colleagues
c. Using vivid, entertaining language when writing a story for young students
d. Using humor to request new privileges from one's parents

71. A class reads an essay about the benefits to youth of pet ownership. The author's position is very clear: she believes young people should be given the responsibility of taking care of pets. The author cites facts, research studies, and statistics to strengthen her position. This type of writing is called:

a. Expository
b. Narrative
c. Persuasive
d. Didactic

72. In the seven steps readers can follow for evaluating the argument by an author of persuasive or argumentative writing, what is accurate about the fifth, sixth, and seventh steps?

a. Authors strengthen their arguments by omitting detracting information.
b. Authors persuade readers better by appealing to emotion than using logic.
c. Author arguments are valid if reasoning is logical, with sequential points.
d. Authors can produce credible arguments which are not necessarily valid.

73. Among seven steps a reader can take to evaluate an author's argument in persuasive writing, which of the first four steps should the reader take *first*?

a. Evaluate the author's objectivity regarding the issue.
b. Judge how relevant the supporting evidence provided is.
c. Identify the author's assumptions regarding the issue.
d. Identify what supporting evidence the author offers.

74. The teacher and her students brainstorm a list of talents, skills, and specialized knowledge belonging to members of the class. Some of the items on the list include how to make a soufflé, how to juggle, and how to teach a dog to do tricks. One student knows a great deal about spiders, and another knows about motorcycles. The teacher asks the students to each write an essay about something they are good at or know a great deal about. What kind of essay is she asking the students to produce?

a. Cause and effect
b. Compare/contrast
c. Expository
d. Argumentative

Copyright © Mometrix Media. You have been licensed one copy of this document for personal use only. Any other reproduction or redistribution is strictly prohibited. All rights reserved.
This content is provided for test preparation purposes only and does not imply an endorsement by Mometrix of any particular political, scientific, or religious point of view.

Educating All Learners and Professional Practice

75. Which of the following examples best demonstrates an intensive intervention plan for a student whose assessment results show she is performing below benchmark levels in decoding consonant blends?

a. Sending home leveled readers containing numerous consonant blends for the student to read with family members
b. Requiring the student to complete independent activities related to consonant blends during the daily word work station
c. Adding 15 minutes of small-group instruction on consonant blends four times per week
d. Teaching a whole-class lesson on consonant blends, followed by multiple independent practice activities

76. Which statement is a key tenet of Marie Clay's literacy processing theory?

a. Children have differing prior knowledge and previous experiences and take different paths to literacy development.
b. Literacy development is enhanced when children learn to write after developing basic reading skills.
c. Emergent readers learn best using large-group instruction, where they have models of proficient readers to emulate.
d. Children learn to read best with a whole-language approach to instruction, with little emphasis on assessment.

77. What is true about speech or language delays and disorders?

a. Delays and disorders both involve abnormal language development sequences.
b. The only difference between delays and disorders is the severity of the problem.
c. Speech or language disorders are more common than speech or language delays.
d. Speech or language delays always involve slower language development rates.

78. Regarding speech pre-production learning activities that teachers can use with ELL students to encourage them to speak English, which of the following is accurate?

a. Choral readings afford advantages for beginning ELLs.
b. Echo reading is not spontaneous and thus not useful.
c. Shared reading and writing will not promote speech.
d. Singing is vocal but otherwise irrelevant to speaking.

79. A teacher uses a mixture of whole-group and small-group reading instruction. Which of the following activities would be the best choice for a whole-group lesson rather than small-group or individualized instruction?

a. Practice applying specific phonics skills
b. Independent reading of unfamiliar texts
c. Analyzing character development after the teacher reads a novel aloud
d. Spelling patterns

80. Which of the following statements is typically true of literature circles?

a. All students within a classroom read and discuss the same book.
b. Teachers predetermine the questions and concepts that will be discussed.
c. Students have choices about the books they read.
d. Groups remain static throughout the year.

Copyright © Mometrix Media. You have been licensed one copy of this document for personal use only. Any other reproduction or redistribution is strictly prohibited. All rights reserved.
This content is provided for test preparation purposes only and does not imply an endorsement by Mometrix of any particular political, scientific, or religious point of view.

81. In the tiered response to intervention (RTI) approach, what has US Department of Education research found to be a best practice for reading instruction?

a. Give all students assessment-based differentiated reading instruction in Tier 1.
b. Give all students the same reading instruction in Tier 1 and differentiate in Tier 2.
c. Give all students differentiated screening; differentiate based on results, not tiers.
d. Give all students the same reading instruction in Tiers 1 and 2, and differentiate in Tier 3.

82. Within a comprehensive literacy program, which of the following descriptions most reflects the nature of small-group differentiated reading instruction?

a. Students have access to ongoing, direct teacher contact while interacting with peers.
b. The teaching and learning of literacy are accomplished through individual interaction.
c. The knowledge of literacy is accumulated through contributions from multiple voices.
d. Students accomplish their learning of literacy through completely independent work.

83. Research into instructional strategies for teaching sight words to students with moderate and severe intellectual disabilities has found which of the following?

a. Traditional approaches are effective for generalization.
b. Some orthographic approaches are better than others.
c. Classroom acquisition outpaces community acquisition.
d. Community-based instruction promotes generalization.

84. Among practices for differentiating reading instruction, which of these represents a valid one?

a. Materials used for read-alouds should be for fun and not common teaching texts.
b. Teachers should instruct the whole class uniformly by using the same single text.
c. Teachers should reserve enough class time for students to read at comfort levels.
d. To reach all student reading levels, teachers should base each unit upon the text.

85. Of the following, what is most characteristic of a skills-focused lesson structure as an alternative to differentiating reading instruction?

a. The lessons move at a slower pace.
b. The lessons are teacher-centered.
c. The lessons vary in skills by group.
d. The lessons only use small groups.

86. Which choice is correct regarding flexible grouping for reading instruction within and across classrooms?

a. Flexible grouping within the classroom is a homogeneous format.
b. Flexible grouping across classrooms has a heterogeneous format.
c. Flexible grouping within the classroom prohibits added resources.
d. Flexible grouping across classrooms can vary teachers for reading.

87. What have research studies found about computer-assisted instruction (CAI) programs for teaching reading and communication skills to students with various disabilities?

a. These programs increase reading skills but decrease interaction.
b. Multimedia software plus scaffolding teach this population less.
c. CAI with the Nonverbal Reading Approach was the most useful.
d. Student differences make individualizing instruction paramount.

Copyright © Mometrix Media. You have been licensed one copy of this document for personal use only. Any other reproduction or redistribution is strictly prohibited. All rights reserved.
This content is provided for test preparation purposes only and does not imply an endorsement by Mometrix of any particular political, scientific, or religious point of view.

88. In implementing a new school reading program, school leaders and leadership teams must rise to the challenge of managing teacher "domestication" of the new program—i.e., altering its design to do it their own way, which frequently decreases its effectiveness—when during its implementation?

a. During the third year of its implementation
b. During the first year of its implementation
c. During the second year of implementation
d. During the fourth year of implementation

89. Which of these does the NEA recommend to promote research-based strategies for developing school partnerships with families and communities at the national level?

a. Policy forums and conferences should include provisions for partnerships, but legislative and policy proposals should not.
b. Educators and families must advocate with federal legislators for partnerships, but these do not belong in federal law.
c. Members of the NEA should disseminate recommended partnership strategies to non-members, not fellow members.
d. School reform initiatives should center around the subject of partnerships among schools, families, and communities.

90. A group of students in a fourth-grade classroom is consistently falling below benchmarks for reading fluency development when compared to their grade-level peers. These students meet twice a week for focused fluency instruction with a reading specialist. This is an example of which type of intervention related to language and literacy development?

a. Tier I response to intervention (RTI)
b. Tier II response to intervention (RTI)
c. Tier III response to intervention (RTI)
d. Individualized education program (IEP)

Copyright © Mometrix Media. You have been licensed one copy of this document for personal use only. Any other reproduction or redistribution is strictly prohibited. All rights reserved.
This content is provided for test preparation purposes only and does not imply an endorsement by Mometrix of any particular political, scientific, or religious point of view.

Answer Key and Explanations for Test #2

Foundations of Reading

1. D: When completing a running record, a teacher records the number of words the student reads correctly out of the total number of words in the text. This is used to calculate the accuracy rate, which helps to determine if the text is at the student's frustration, instructional, or independent reading level. Authentic assessment tasks provide opportunities for students to complete reading and writing activities while solving real-world problems rather than opportunities to calculate the accuracy rate when reading a text. Rubrics are used to evaluate students' performances based on multiple criteria on assignments and assessments, but they are not used to calculate accuracy rate, either. Guided reading observations may help the teacher determine if a text is much too easy or much too difficult for a student to read independently, but without the running record, the exact accuracy rate cannot be determined.

2. B: By taking a whole word and breaking it into its individual sounds, the students are practicing segmenting. Blending is the opposite process, where students take individual sounds and combine them to form a whole word. Phoneme isolation refers to identifying the beginning, middle, or ending sound in a word. Phoneme identification refers to identifying a common sound in a group of words with either the same beginning, middle, or ending sound.

3. C: Research has shown that reading and writing are interrelated processes, and literacy development is enhanced when they are taught together. Even very young children can be encouraged to use writing to communicate, though their early attempts at writing may be scribbles. This helps children develop an understanding that print carries meaning, and it also assists with development of directionality and other concepts of print. Similarly, children learn concepts of print and skills that they use in their writing by seeing them modeled in the books they read.

4. B: Experts find that narrating ELL students' actions, i.e., linguistic encoding, helps encourage them to speak English (A), that teachers should assign activities that include hands-on learning (B), and that the activities they assign should be meaningful (C). They also find that teachers should focus on which language function the students must apply to complete a lesson, not just that they complete it (D).

5. B: Typically, guided practice follows modeling. Independent practice and application would then follow the guided practice, and generalization would come last. Feedback should be provided throughout multiple levels of instruction, particularly during the practice phases.

6. D: A consonant digraph is a group of two or three consonants that form a new consonant sound when combined. The *ch* in the word *cheek* forms a new sound. The other choices contain consonant blends. In consonant blends, two or three consonants blend together, but each individual letter sound is still heard.

7. B: Decodable texts use many words containing previously taught phonics skills, allowing readers to practice those skills in context while reading new books. They can be one component found in classrooms that use explicit phonics instruction. Choice A describes predictable books, which rely more on patterns in language rather than phonics skills, to assist readers with decoding. Because most words in decodable texts contain previously learned phonics skills, they do not often have content-related vocabulary words with more complex spelling patterns. Additionally, the focus is

Copyright © Mometrix Media. You have been licensed one copy of this document for personal use only. Any other reproduction or redistribution is strictly prohibited. All rights reserved.
This content is provided for test preparation purposes only and does not imply an endorsement by Mometrix of any particular political, scientific, or religious point of view.

on using decodable words rather than on complex plot development, so they may not be appropriate for close reading activities.

8. B: Although the illustrations themselves are visual images, using the information available from them to inform reading is not using a visual cue (A). Word appearance and length, familiar-looking phrases, and word-initial letters or phonemes—i.e., visual aspects of the verbal text itself—are examples of visual cues. Because the student uses information from illustrations, he or she uses a meaning cue (B). A structural cue (C) would involve using knowledge of syntax (sentence structure) to inform correct reading. A graphophonic cue (D) would involve using knowledge of sound-to-letter correspondences.

9. C: Orthographic processing refers to recognizing letter patterns that make up words or word parts. For example, a student may see the word *sight* and immediately recognize the *ight* pattern. The ability to separate spoken words into component sounds is a part of phonological awareness. Alphabetic principle is the understanding that each letter makes a predictable sound. Receptive language involves understanding spoken words.

10. C: While it is true that phonemic awareness is a listening and speaking skill rather than a reading and writing skill (A), it is equally true that children develop phonemic awareness better when instruction combines print with speech sounds (B). This helps children realize how speech sounds and printed letters connect and apply this insight. However, just including print is not sufficient (C). Teachers should also point to printed letters while saying them aloud to draw children's attention to sound-letter connections (D).

11. B: When students combine the initial sound in a word with the remainder of the word, they are blending the onset and rime. Syllabification involves breaking a word into syllables. A word may have one or more syllables. Phoneme isolation involves identifying either the beginning, middle, or ending sound in a word. Segmentation involves breaking a word into its individual sounds.

12. C: Children often invent spellings during early learning. Though vowels are needed to decode words, these invented spellings frequently omit vowels (A); therefore, children need a great deal of practice to hear vowel sounds in words. Children can discriminate long vowel sounds more easily than short vowel sounds, not vice versa (B). Hence (though many phonics programs start with short vowels), phonological discrimination exercises should often focus on discriminating long vowels before short vowels, not vice versa (D).

13. D: None; irregular sight words cannot generally be decoded. Readers must learn to recognize these as whole words on sight. They either have irregular spelling or do not follow typical phonic patterns, so an attempt at decoding may ultimately mislead the reader. Segmenting them into syllables or using a phonemic approach are ineffective strategies to aid a reader in recognizing a sight word because these approaches depend on rules a sight word doesn't follow. Word families group words that share common patterns of consonants and vowels. The spelling of those words is, therefore, regular because they follow a predictable pattern. Sight words that are irregular, do not follow a predictable pattern, and must be instantaneously recognized for writing fluency. Decoding is not useful.

14. C: The act of decoding involves first recognizing the sounds individual letters and letter groups make and then blending the sounds to read the word. A child decoding the word *spin*, for example, would first pronounce *sp/i/n* as individual sound units. She then would repeat the sounds, smoothly blending them. Because decoding involves understanding letters and their sounds, it is sometimes known as the alphabetic principle.

Copyright © Mometrix Media. You have been licensed one copy of this document for personal use only. Any other reproduction or redistribution is strictly prohibited. All rights reserved.
This content is provided for test preparation purposes only and does not imply an endorsement by Mometrix of any particular political, scientific, or religious point of view.

15. C: The teacher is demonstrating a think-aloud, or sharing her thinking process as she uses a reading strategy. In this example, she explains her thoughts as she uses context clues to determine the meaning of an unknown word. Mental images and visualizations both refer to the pictures that readers get in their minds when they read. Predictions are logical guesses about what might happen in a text.

16. D: It offers a systematic approach to untangling the wide variety of vowel sounds when an unfamiliar word is encountered. Code knowledge, also called orthographic tendencies, is a helpful approach to decoding a word when multiple pronunciation possibilities exist. For example, in the words *toe, go, though,* and *low*, the long O sound is written in a variety of ways. A code knowledge approach teaches a reader to first try a short vowel sound. If that doesn't help, the reader should consider the different ways the vowel or vowel groups can be pronounced, based on what he knows about other words.

17. A: The type or pattern of error most damaging to reading proficiency is substituting words with similar appearances or spelling but completely different meanings, because this shows a lack of reading for meaning. Substituting synonyms (B) shows some comprehension of word meaning. Substituting like parts of speech (C) shows some comprehension of grammar and syntax. Substituting correct words or closer approximations for errors based on information from the sentence context (D) shows skills in both reading for meaning and self-correction.

18. A: A morpheme is the smallest unit of language with meaning. An example is the prefix *pre*, which means before. *Pre* cannot be broken down any further without losing its meaning. The smallest unit of speech is a phoneme. A grapheme is a letter or group of letters representing a single sound. A syllable is a unit of spoken language in a word that contains a single uninterrupted sound.

19. D: In choice D, the root word, *argue*, drops its *e* before the suffix is added. The correct spelling of the new word is *argument*. In the other options, the root words remain unchanged when the suffix is added.

20. C: Word walls should be flexible, meaning words can be removed if students have mastered them, and new words can be added as they are introduced. It is also helpful if the words on word walls are removable, so students can take them to other areas of the room when they are using them for reading and writing activities. Choice A is incorrect because there are many types of words that can be included on word walls, including content-related vocabulary, academic vocabulary, and high-frequency words. Choice B is incorrect because words can be displayed on word walls for different reasons. For example, words containing the same root can be displayed to help students see relationships between words. Because word walls can contain different types of words and be used for different purposes, they can be helpful for readers in all stages of reading development.

21. B: Educational research into teaching practices for nonverbal communication is notably lacking; however, teachers who have experimented with lessons (cf. Darn, 2014) have discovered it is best to teach nonverbal communication skills in small chunks (A), using appropriate situations (B) wherein the context of the theme or situation is congruent with the language. They also find that to help students use gestures and expressions to reinforce linguistic meaning, teachers must include drama-based instructional activities that build student confidence (C) and creativity (D).

22. C: The general rule about splitting doubled consonants pertains most to syllabication, i.e., where to divide words up into their component syllables to inform pronunciation and meaning. Structural analysis (A) pertains to dividing words into component parts like prefixes, roots, and suffixes, which may or may not coincide with syllable divisions. Using common spelling patterns (B)

Copyright © Mometrix Media. You have been licensed one copy of this document for personal use only. Any other reproduction or redistribution is strictly prohibited. All rights reserved.
This content is provided for test preparation purposes only and does not imply an endorsement by Mometrix of any particular political, scientific, or religious point of view.

pertains to determining meaning and pronunciation in unfamiliar words by comparing their spelling to the same or similar spellings in familiar words. Using morphemes (D) pertains to identifying the smallest meaningful grammatical units in words, e.g., *-ed* verb endings signify past tense.

23. D: Researchers have found that explicit instruction in phonics does help students at risk for reading failure particularly, but also promotes higher achievement by all students (A). Research supports the use of decodable books (B) early in first grade. Studies find that the kind of text read by students affects the word identification strategies they use (C), and also that prior student literacy knowledge (indicated by reading readiness assessment), as well as using decodable texts early, contribute to developing understanding of sound-spelling relationships (D).

24. A: According to the National Research Council (Snow, Burns, and Griffin, 1998), phonological awareness is the general ability to distinguish speech sounds from their meanings, whereas phonemic awareness is a more specific ability to distinguish individual speech sounds, i.e., phonemes, within words. Hence phonemic awareness is the most sophisticated level of phonological awareness (D). Therefore, choice B and C are also incorrect.

25. D: Research shows that phonics instruction is more effective than no phonics instruction, and also that it is more effective when it is systematic and explicit then when it is not (A). Research also shows that it is equally effective for children of all socioeconomic levels (B), that it is more effective when introduced in kindergarten or first grade (C), and that it is more effective when it helps students understand why they are learning letter-sound relationships and helps them apply this learning (D) to reading and writing.

26. D: If a student reads aloud without any vocal changes to identify text punctuation (A), this is a sign of difficulty with decoding words. Students often exhibit difficulties with comprehension by leaving out, glossing over, or minimizing details (B) when reading. When students insert additional words that are not already in the text (C), it is a sign that the student could be rushing through the text too quickly. Having issues with connecting ideas within a text passage (D) is a common sign of difficulty with reading retention.

27. D: Automaticity in reading refers to one's ability to decode written words quickly and accurately. This is essential for building reading fluency, as it allows young readers to focus their attention on understanding the whole text rather than sounding out individual words. Frequent practice and assessment of automaticity in the early childhood classroom are essential for gauging reading proficiency levels and identifying areas of need for additional support. One effective strategy for evaluating automaticity involves timing students as they individually read aloud from a grade-level text. This method allows teachers to determine students' speed in correctly identifying and comprehending words in a text, providing measurable data on each individual's progress. In the above example, the teacher utilizes this approach to assess automaticity by having students individually read a passage aloud from *The Secret Garden* for one minute. In doing so, the teacher is able to determine how many words each student read, how many errors were made, and how many words per minute the student accurately recognizes and comprehends, thus providing a comprehensive assessment of each student's automaticity skills.

28. A: Incorporating new and complex academic language into meaningful contexts is integral to promoting acquisition and retention. Doing so provides students with a framework for reference when encountering unfamiliar vocabulary, thus facilitating their comprehension. An effective strategy for achieving this involves providing students with authentic tasks focused on newly learned academic language. Authentic tasks are those which prompt students to apply new

Copyright © Mometrix Media. You have been licensed one copy of this document for personal use only. Any other reproduction or redistribution is strictly prohibited. All rights reserved.
This content is provided for test preparation purposes only and does not imply an endorsement by Mometrix of any particular political, scientific, or religious point of view.

concepts in real-world situations, thus strengthening their personal connections to make learning relevant and meaningful. In the given scenario, assigning students to create their own version of a constitution provides an authentic opportunity for utilizing newly acquired academic language in an engaging and meaningful context, thus reinforcing their understanding and internalization of the new vocabulary.

29. C: Reading comprehension and fluency development is reliant on students' ability to apply contextual analysis skills to determine the meaning of unfamiliar vocabulary words. Contextual analysis, as it relates to language and literacy development, involves locating and using clues within a text to infer the meaning of new vocabulary. Various strategies can effectively promote the development of students' contextual analysis skills. For example, students can look for definition words related to new vocabulary within a text, deduce meaning from pictures or illustrations, or search for clue words, such as synonyms, antonyms, or explanations of unfamiliar terms. By guiding students in locating clue words within a text to decipher the meaning of unfamiliar vocabulary, the teacher in this scenario can effectively develop students' contextual analysis skills by prompting them to utilize context clues in making educated guesses about the meaning of new vocabulary words.

Text Comprehension and Analysis

30. B: The best model a teacher can provide to students in this situation is effective reading strategies that result in better overall comprehension. Choice B effectively accomplishes this by first reading for the main idea, which is easier to grasp than smaller details that can be misleading or unrelated to the point of the passage. Reading, then re-reading is a great skill to show students to help them know to approach the text and be willing to put more time in to understand the passage more fully, rather than just looking for information for a particular answer. Choice A is wrong because while learning to underline meaningful information in a passage is useful, going straight to the place where the answers are located does not help model the overall search for information. Choice C is wrong because it pertains to general test-taking tips and is not directly related to reading comprehension or use of textual evidence. Choice D is wrong because it models weak practices. It is generally not a good idea to complete an organizational framework until you are well-acquainted with a passage. The whole text should be read first, then when the overall idea is understood, someone can go back and fill in a story map.

31. A: A story map outlines the main elements of the story, including the characters, setting, conflict, plot, and resolution. Recording these elements will assist the student in remembering and analyzing the story after it has been read. If the student has retention issues, he or she may not recall the story elements even after reading the story twice or listening to an audio version. A KWL chart can be used to activate prior knowledge and help the student reflect on what was learned, but it does not outline the story elements needed to analyze plot.

32. B: Figurative language involves the use of words and phrases that differ from their literal meanings. The expression in choice B means that the wet snow covered the ground, not that it was literally a wet blanket. It is an example of a metaphor, which is one type of figurative language. The other options contain some descriptive words and phrases, but they have literal meanings.

33. C: Picture walks are frequently used to activate students' prior knowledge. When readers look at the pictures, they make connections between the content of the new texts and what they already know from other texts or life experiences. These connections can spark interest in the stories and deepen comprehension. Teachers may encourage the use of syntactic cues during guided reading groups, but this is not typically part of a picture walk. Setting a purpose for reading is another

Copyright © Mometrix Media. You have been licensed one copy of this document for personal use only. Any other reproduction or redistribution is strictly prohibited. All rights reserved.
This content is provided for test preparation purposes only and does not imply an endorsement by Mometrix of any particular political, scientific, or religious point of view.

beneficial prereading activity, but it is not always a part of a picture walk either. Metacognitive skills, which assist students with self-monitoring during reading, are also beneficial, but they are not typically the focus of a picture walk.

34. D: Text structure refers to how a text is organized. Different text structures are used depending on the purpose for writing, and cause/effect, compare/contrast, and time-order text structures are all commonly used in nonfiction texts. Literary devices are techniques authors use in their writing to set a certain mood, emphasize a point, convey a description, or more. Literary elements refer to parts of texts, such as characters, setting, plot, conflict, and resolution. Genres refer to specific categories of texts, such as fantasies.

35. D: Reciprocal teaching is an activity in which students gradually take over the role of the teacher in small groups to discuss texts. The students lead discussions focused on four main reading strategies: summarizing, questioning, predicting, and clarifying. The remaining options are also reading strategies, but they are not typically the focus of reciprocal teaching activities.

36. A: Generally, the sequence of instruction is as follows: explicit instruction, modeling, guided practice, independent practice and application, and generalization. The teacher has already completed the explicit instruction, modeling, and guided practice portion of the sequence. Therefore, independent practice and application would come next. Choice A best demonstrates this stage of instruction. Reteaching is only necessary if informal or formal assessments indicate that students did not learn the skill after the first attempt at instruction, which is not indicated in this example. Choice C represents the generalization stage, which typically comes after students have had independent practice with the skill. A formal assessment, such as a test, should also come after independent practice opportunities.

37. B: Caleb is stating that nobody likes meatloaf after observing that a small sample of the school population does not appear to like it. He is drawing conclusions based on insufficient data, which is an overgeneralization. An illogical conclusion occurs when someone draws conclusions about the relationships between two things without data supporting the relationship. Personal bias occurs when conclusions are based on personal opinions rather than data. Circular reasoning occurs when someone supports a claim by restating the same claim rather than by providing new data.

38. B: This book contains elements of fantasy due to the time travel, and it contains elements of historical fiction with the characters' participation in the American Revolution. Choice A is incorrect because it is not a story passed down over time, so it is not a folktale. Additionally, while some portions of the story may seem realistic, the time traveling element makes it more fantasy than realistic fiction. Choice C is incorrect because the story doesn't focus on a moral or contain talking animals. Choice D is incorrect because it is not a folktale.

39. C: Aesthetic response refers to a reader's personal interactions with a text. Rather than recalling information about the text, aesthetic response is personalized and based on the reader's own thoughts, feelings, and reactions. Choice C asks the readers to describe how a certain part of the story made them feel; therefore, it is focused on their aesthetic responses to the text. The other questions can be answered using information contained within the story rather than the readers' own personal reactions.

40. C: Close reading involves multiple readings of the same text, with students analyzing different layers of the text each time. Students read the texts independently, with no picture walks or pre-teaching beforehand. Close reading is designed to help students become actively involved in the reading process and develop deeper understandings of what they have read. Guided reading is done

Copyright © Mometrix Media. You have been licensed one copy of this document for personal use only. Any other reproduction or redistribution is strictly prohibited. All rights reserved.
This content is provided for test preparation purposes only and does not imply an endorsement by Mometrix of any particular political, scientific, or religious point of view.

in small groups, with teachers focusing on targeted skills based on students' needs. Additionally, picture walks are often done in guided reading groups. SQ3R is a strategy often used to help students comprehend textbook readings. It involves students doing a quick survey of the text, followed by identification of questions about the text. Students then read the text, recite it in their own words, and review the main idea. Scanning involves reading quickly to identify specific information.

41. D: Literal comprehension is what text states overtly, e.g., story characters, event sequences, stated facts, etc. Choices A and B are examples of literal comprehension responses. Inferential comprehension is deeper or implicit meaning not explicitly stated, which readers must infer by considering text and drawing conclusions, e.g., unstated main ideas, cause-and-effect relationships, generalizations, and predictions. Choice C is an example of an inferential comprehension response. Evaluative comprehension requires readers to form opinions after analyzing text information. Choice D is an example of an evaluative comprehension response.

42. B: Inferring requires readers to use clues rather than explicit evidence to determine the author's meaning. Choice B requires students to use the character's statements to infer how he or she felt at the time. Choice A requires students to evaluate the writing. Choice C requires students to make a prediction. Choice D requires students to make a text-to-text connection.

43. B: The Directed Reading Thinking Activity, i.e., DRTA, is a comprehension strategy that helps students ask questions about text, make predictions about it, and then read to confirm or deny predictions. Gist (A) is a comprehension strategy that helps students identify the main idea, paraphrase, and summarize text. The Fishbowl (C) is an instructional strategy that helps students participate in classroom discussions. Cornell Notes (D) is an instructional strategy that helps students take notes, read text carefully, organize, and summarize information.

44. B: A persuasive essay takes a strong position about a controversial topic and offers factual evidence to support this position. The goal of a persuasive paper is to convince the audience that the claim is true based on the evidence provided.

45. B: Literal comprehension is an understanding of what is actually stated in the text by the author. Questions of this type involve recalling information and often answer who, what, when, where, or why. Affective comprehension refers to readers' personal reactions to texts based on their individual experiences, prior knowledge, and preferences. Inferential comprehension is a deeper level of comprehension than literal comprehension. It requires readers to make inferences when the answers to questions are not directly stated in the text. Evaluative comprehension is a deeper level than both literal and inferential comprehension. It involves using prior knowledge and textual evidence to form judgments about the text.

46. D: Wallace et al. (*Reading Horizons,* V48.1, 2007) recommend four instructional strategies that use writing to improve student reading comprehension. About/point (C) is a summarizing strategy that helps students learn to differentiate main ideas from supporting details. Cubing (D) is a strategy that helps students learn to see information from various perspectives. Four square graphic organizer (B) is an organizational strategy that helps students make connections in content across the curriculum. Read, respond, revisit, discuss (A) is a strategy that helps students comprehend text by integrating reading, writing, and social interaction.

47. D: Schema theory suggests that when people encounter new concepts, the newly learned knowledge gets organized into units called schemata. When they encounter related information in the future, they access their existing schemata to make sense of it. Therefore, a KWL chart, which

Copyright © Mometrix Media. You have been licensed one copy of this document for personal use only. Any other reproduction or redistribution is strictly prohibited. All rights reserved.
This content is provided for test preparation purposes only and does not imply an endorsement by Mometrix of any particular political, scientific, or religious point of view.

helps students relate a topic to existing knowledge, best supports schema theory. The remaining types of graphic organizers support reading development but do not specifically require students to activate prior knowledge.

48. C: If the author's purpose were to inform (A), the text would present facts, explain phenomena or events, or give directions. To entertain (B), the text would contain humor, satire, adventure, suspense, horror, etc. To persuade (C), the text would present a position or point(s), support it or them with evidence, and raise and refute a counterpoint(s). To analyze (D), the text would break a subject or issue into its component parts, examine these, discuss their relationships and interactions, etc.

49. B: An integral aspect of cultivating reading comprehension and critical analysis skills involves the ability to interact with a text, recognize key elements, make inferences, and formulate opinions. This enables students to engage meaningfully in reading, formulate connections between ideas, and integrate information. Close readings are an effective strategy for encouraging students to delve deeply into a text. This activity prompts students to thoroughly examine and analyze a text, often by marking symbols throughout to signify various elements, such as unfamiliar vocabulary, questions or thoughts, and key information. Performing close readings is beneficial in helping students focus intentionally on specific aspects of a text to derive meaning, strengthening reading comprehension and critical analysis skills. In the above example, the student's markings throughout the assigned text to signify unfamiliar vocabulary, key information, and questions indicate a close reading activity.

50. B: Implementing effective pre-reading strategies is essential to helping students navigate complex and often content-specific informational texts. Such strategies typically engage students' prior knowledge, which serves as a framework for reference when students begin reading to foster personal connections and strengthen understanding. Effective pre-reading strategies also encourage meaningful interaction with a text, as this helps focus students' attention on specific information as they read, thus promoting deeper analysis and improved comprehension. KWL charts are effective in achieving both goals. This activity includes three columns, categorized as what students know about a given topic prior to reading, what they want to know, and what they learned after reading. Having students record what they already know about a topic, such as agriculture, taps into their prior knowledge and experiences. Prompting students to list what they want to learn before reading focuses their attention on looking for specific information as they read, thus promoting greater analysis and active engagement with the text. By having students in this scenario complete the first two columns of a KWL chart before reading a text about agriculture, this teacher can establish a strong foundation for promoting students' comprehension and analysis skills.

51. D: Providing students with effective graphic organizers promotes comprehension of complex informational texts. This learning tool allows students to organize their thoughts while reading, focus on specific details, and visualize important information for greater retention. Graphic organizers are versatile and can be tailored to align with nearly any style of text. In the given scenario, the teacher plans to assign an expository text about different kinds of rocks and their characteristics. Considering each paragraph in the passage focuses on a specific type of rock, an outline would be the most suitable style of graphic organizer. This format will allow students to specify the main idea of each paragraph and record important information, thus focusing their attention on categorizing the names of each kind of rock and their unique features.

52. A: Reading comprehension is typically categorized into three levels: literal, inferential, and evaluative, with evaluative requiring the most complex degree of thought. This level entails the

Copyright © Mometrix Media. You have been licensed one copy of this document for personal use only. Any other reproduction or redistribution is strictly prohibited. All rights reserved.
This content is provided for test preparation purposes only and does not imply an endorsement by Mometrix of any particular political, scientific, or religious point of view.

ability to connect reading content to previous experiences and to formulate personal thoughts and opinions about the information presented. To develop this skill, it is important that educators ask students questions that prompt them to think critically about their own interpretations of a text. For example, asking students whether they agree with an author's viewpoint and encouraging them to elaborate on their opinion fosters independent critical thinking to evaluate the text based on their own judgements. By asking such a question after having students read an informational text, this teacher can leverage students' higher order thinking skills to promote deeper analysis and comprehension.

Oral and Written Communication

53. B: Aidan is writing to convince the cafeteria manager to act on a specific request, and he supports his request with reasons. This is indicative of persuasive writing. When authors write to inform, they share information about their topics to teach readers new things. When authors write to entertain, they write to provide readers with enjoyable experiences. When authors write to describe, they write to share descriptive details about their topics.

54. D: According to experts, teachers can model appropriate listening and speaking behaviors for students when they facilitate book discussions and during everyday conversations with them (A), when giving instruction to both whole classes and small groups (B), in one-to-one conversations they have with students and during classroom media discussions (C), and by thinking aloud specifically about the content they are teaching (D).

55. A: Choice A is Chomsky's theory of Universal Grammar, which essentially posits that all languages use a structure and that these structural rules are innate to humans. Put another way, humans are innately capable of and inclined to acquire the rules of language. Choice B refers to another theory, the Natural Order Hypothesis, which describes a predictable order in language acquisition, which is universal to language acquisition. Choices C and D do not describe any current theories of acquisition.

56. D: Synthesis involves gathering information from multiple sources and combining it to make meaning, as students are doing when they write their research reports on sustainable farming practices. As students collect information from each source, they also consider how their initial thoughts on the topic have changed. Evaluating involves making a judgment about something. Inferring involves using clues in the text to make meaning rather than using information that is directly stated. Drawing conclusions involves making judgements based on inferences.

57. C: Teachers need to advise students that when they take research notes on information sources, they should note all details of the source material rather than taking more generalized notes (A), and differentiate clearly not only between quotations and paraphrases (B), but also between their own paraphrases and their own commentaries (D). Essentially, they must clearly differentiate among direct quotations from sources, their own paraphrases of statements in sources, and their own commentaries on those source statements (C).

58. A: The student is adjusting his language according to his current social situation. When speaking to a friend, he uses informal language. When presenting a report in front of the class and teacher, he switches to more formal language. Cultural context refers to the ways that messages are delivered and received based on differing cultural backgrounds and norms. Contextual clues are clues in a text that assist readers with determining the meanings of unknown words. Personal context refers to how communication is affected by an individual's age, gender, educational background, and other personal factors.

Copyright © Mometrix Media. You have been licensed one copy of this document for personal use only. Any other reproduction or redistribution is strictly prohibited. All rights reserved.
This content is provided for test preparation purposes only and does not imply an endorsement by Mometrix of any particular political, scientific, or religious point of view.

59. B: The students will employ brainstorming and a compare/contrast strategy. Brainstorming is a prewriting activity in which an individual or group responds to a specific question by considering any and all responses that arise without editing, prioritizing, or selecting. Once the brainstorming session is complete, students look at the results and eliminate any responses that are not useful, then group and prioritize the remaining responses. In this example, the students are having a collaborative learning experience in that they are brainstorming together; however, collaborative learning is not a strategy per se, but is the outcome of a strategy. The students are also employing a compare/contrast strategy in that they are looking both at how the two writing styles share common elements and how they are distinct.

60. C: Students will do online research about the cultural, economic, or political events that were occurring during the specific time about which they've written. By researching the historic setting that surrounded the events their interviewee discussed, students are simultaneously broadening their understanding of the context and working in a different content area.

61. D: The teacher is considering the cultural load the student is facing. Cultural load is concerned with how the relationship between language and culture can help or hinder learning. By using the Korean folk tale, the teacher offered the child the opportunity to learn new words in a context that was culturally familiar. By demonstrating respect for her student's culture, she helped lighten the cultural load.

62. A: Keyword substitution involves replacing a phoneme in key words of song lyrics or other common phrases and sayings. This gives children practice in wordplay and is entertaining. After singing the revised lyrics, teachers can discuss with children how changing one phoneme changed the meanings of words in the song. Changing /r/ to /ʃ/ in "Row, row, row your boat" (A) is an example. Choice B transposes the two nouns in the lyric. Keyword substitution refers to substituting different phonemes in key words, not substituting different whole words or transposing existing words. Choice C quotes the first line of Lewis Carroll's poem "Jabberwocky," famous for using many nonsense words. Choice D uses the same song as choice A but deletes initial phonemes rather than substituting.

63. C: Various researchers have found that people spend 70 percent of waking hours communicating, and three-quarters of that time is spent listening and speaking. In total, communication time consists of 30 percent speaking, 16 percent reading, 9 percent writing, and 45 percent listening. Yet other researchers have found that schools have spent 12 years formally teaching writing, 6-8 years teaching reading, 1-2 years teaching speaking, and 0-6 months teaching listening.

64. D: Varying levels of explicit instruction, assigning small groups, and varying amounts of writing instruction time (A) reflects the principle of incorporating differentiated instruction. Allowing enough time for systematic writing opportunities in all content subjects as well as ELA classes (B) reflects the principle of integrating teaching writing across the curriculum. Incorporating reasons and methods for explicit writing instruction (C) reflects the principle of including rationales and methods of explicit writing instruction. Effective organization, spelling, vocabulary, syntax, etc., for different subjects (D) reflect the principle of teaching knowledge that enables more effective writing.

65. D: During a virtual tour, teachers can have students find more information by visiting both websites and computer labs (A); locate experts in fields pertinent to classroom study, including those willing to speak directly with students (B); and not only record calls, but also connect a projector, speaker, or other sound device, enabling students to hear both ends of the teacher's

Copyright © Mometrix Media. You have been licensed one copy of this document for personal use only. Any other reproduction or redistribution is strictly prohibited. All rights reserved.
This content is provided for test preparation purposes only and does not imply an endorsement by Mometrix of any particular political, scientific, or religious point of view.

conversation (C). Teachers can plan for Q&A sessions near the ends of conversations and have students direct these by asking their own questions (D).

66. D: A few principles are important to keep in mind when trying to achieve clarity in a written speech. Grammar and word choice should be accurate, but the speechwriter should keep in mind that each sentence will be spoken to an audience rather than read by one, so choice D is correct. Choice A is incorrect because the speechwriter must define the purpose of the speech before writing or delivering it. Choice B is incorrect because prioritizing audience engagement will by necessity involve logical organization, as audiences will not be able to follow a poorly organized speech. Choice C is incorrect because making an outline first gives the speechwriter a structure on which to build an engaging speech. Rather than hurting attention, a clear outline increases the chances that audiences will be able to follow all of the points made.

67. B: Relational messages, as opposed to content messages, are concerned with the relationship between a speaker and a recipient rather than with the overt subject of the communication. They may convey belonging, respect, or disapproval, among other things. They are frequently largely or entirely nonverbal; because of this, they may be supported with verbal feedback to confirm them. The content of the message, "Should I come over after work?" is a logistical request. If a speaker leans forward to touch a recipient who is weeping, the relational message is "Do you need my support?" The recipient might respond with a nod and a grateful look, or might clarify the speaker's offer by saying, "I won't be good company, but you can come."

68. A: When a speaker is making a statement or answering a question from the audience, s/he should not take three or more minutes to get to the point, which will lose listener attention. Getting off the subject has the same effect. However, speakers should not be afraid to pause before answering audience questions (B): this gives them time to formulate a clear response, as well as demonstrating to their listeners that they are thoughtful and in control. Including too many anecdotes and details (C) is not good: it causes audiences to lose track of the subject/get confused. Similarly, speakers should include necessary information but not all other interesting information. (D): Information overload triggers listeners' brains to shut down due to having more input than they can process.

69. B: Choice B is correct, as natural communication is generally ideal in public speaking, and verbal and nonverbal communication alike should be natural. Choice A is incorrect because speakers should practice their speeches extensively to ensure confidence and ease of delivery; they will not be received as spontaneous in a good way if they stumble, search for words, or stop to consult notes. Choice C is incorrect because the use of humor can be used to engage with the audience and keep their attention. Although too much humor could be distracting, it is a good tool for audience engagement when used appropriately. Choice D is incorrect because random or irrelevant movements (such as hair-twirling, foot-tapping, pencil-tapping, face-rubbing, etc.) will distract the audience rather than engage them.

70. C: When students write for their classmates, they should use language that is more informal and age-appropriate, not more sophisticated (A). Jargon also gives the general impression of confusing language where simpler language would be effective. When describing a procedure to a colleague, especially one who is considered an expert, a writer should not need to use simple language (B), as the colleague will likely understand relevant technical or sophisticated language. When writing for younger children, students should use more vivid and entertaining language (C), including some humor when appropriate. When asking parental permission for more independent activities, students should use language that seems more mature and serious rather than using humor (D).

Copyright © Mometrix Media. You have been licensed one copy of this document for personal use only. Any other reproduction or redistribution is strictly prohibited. All rights reserved.
This content is provided for test preparation purposes only and does not imply an endorsement by Mometrix of any particular political, scientific, or religious point of view.

71. C: The author is hoping to persuade or convince readers to either request a pet and/or the primary care of their pet by providing them with facts as well as by using rhetorical devices such as dispelling opposing arguments.

72. C: In the fifth of seven reader steps for evaluating argumentative writing, readers assess whether the author's argument is complete. Some authors may not present enough supporting evidence. Or they may omit information that detracts from their argument, making their argument incomplete rather than including such detracting material and then refuting it, which makes the argument more complete. The reader's sixth step is to determine the validity of the author's argument. While argumentation may sway reader opinion by influencing reader feelings, valid arguments also use clear, logical reasoning rather than relying solely upon emotional appeals; the points they make follow a sequence, with one leading to the next. The seventh reader step is to decide if the argument is credible. For an argument to be believable it must first be valid.

73. C: The first step the reader should take for evaluating argumentative writing is to identify what assumptions the author has made about the issue s/he discusses in the writing. Assumptions are things that the author accepts without proof. If an author's assumptions are incorrect or illogical, the ensuing argument will be flawed. Readers can be misled by argumentative writing if they do not identify the author's assumptions. The reader's second step is to identify what kinds of evidence the author has offered to support the argument (D). The reader should then take the third step of evaluating how relevant this evidence is (B). The fourth step for the reader is to evaluate how objective the author is about the issue discussed in the writing (A).

74. C: Expository essays are any type of essay in which the writer is providing meaningful information about a topic for the purpose of informing. Most of the topics listed in the example include informational tasks, explaining the process of doing something, such as baking or juggling. Expository essays can use various organizational schemes to help structure the information, such as by comparing and contrasting two things. An expository essay is different from an argumentative essay in that it is not trying to convince the reader of anything, but only trying to inform. Similarly, the purpose of a descriptive essay is to show detail, but not necessarily to inform about how something works.

Educating All Learners and Professional Practice

75. C: Choice C best demonstrates an intensive intervention plan because it includes small-group, targeted instruction at frequent, regularly scheduled times. The remaining options can assist the student with learning consonant blends, but they do not include frequent, regularly scheduled teacher interactions. During these intervention times, the teacher can provide instruction, supervise practice opportunities, offer feedback, monitor progress, and more.

76. A: A key tenet of Marie Clay's theory is the understanding that children take different paths to becoming readers based on differences in prior knowledge and experiences. As a result, teachers must meet the needs of individual learners rather than using a one-size-fits-all approach to instruction. Choice B is incorrect because Clay's theory also explains the interrelationship between reading and writing. Choice C is incorrect because Clay's theory emphasizes the importance of individualized instruction based on students' unique needs and experiences. Choice D is incorrect because frequent observation and data collection are important components of individualized instruction, as they allow teachers to determine students' strengths and needs.

77. D: Speech or language delays and disorders always involve slower language development rates, but not always in the same ways. Speech or language delays involve a normal *sequence* of language

Copyright © Mometrix Media. You have been licensed one copy of this document for personal use only. Any other reproduction or redistribution is strictly prohibited. All rights reserved.
This content is provided for test preparation purposes only and does not imply an endorsement by Mometrix of any particular political, scientific, or religious point of view.

development (A) but at slower rates than normal. Speech or language disorders involve abnormal language development, including development not following the normal sequence. Due to the broken sequence, language development is considered slow as disordered speech prevents children from hitting the appropriate benchmarks on time. Thus, severity is not the only difference (B). Speech or language delays are more common than speech or language disorders, not vice versa (C). In fact, speech or language delays are the most common developmental issue, affecting 5-10 percent of preschoolers.

78. A: Teachers can encourage ELLs to speak English through meaningful activities that include choral readings, which are less daunting than solo readings, give a sense of safety and strength in numbers, and provide the least proficient or confident students with multiple models or partners. Echo reading is useful (B) by modeling correct reading that students emulate. Shared reading and writing promote both understanding and use of English language, thus promoting English speech (C). Singing encourages speech (D) by providing an easier way to vocalize in English through the added structure of melody and rhythm and the ability to memorize lyrics beforehand.

79. C: One of the challenges of large-group instruction is meeting the needs of diverse learners. Reading a novel aloud helps to make the content accessible to all learners. If students were to read it independently, as in choice B, the text would likely not be challenging enough for some readers and too difficult for others. Therefore, basing a comprehension lesson on a book that was read aloud assists all students with participating. While teachers sometimes introduce and practice phonics skills in large groups, students are likely to have differing skill levels in this area. Proficient first-grade readers, for example, may read consonant blends and digraphs with ease, which struggling readers may still be learning the alphabetic principle. Students in a classroom are also likely to have vastly different spelling skills, making the need for differentiation important.

80. C: Although teachers may supply the possible options, students are typically given choices about the books they read for literature circles. This helps maintain interest and engagement throughout the process. Students participate in literature circles in small groups, and there are usually multiple books being read and discussed throughout a classroom. Students are encouraged to lead the discussions and introduce questions and topics for analysis. Additionally, groups may change frequently as students finish books and move on to new texts.

81. A: The federal Department of Education (ED)'s What Works Clearinghouse (WWC) finds the most effective practice in RTI is to give all students differentiated reading instruction in Tier 1 rather than only in Tier 2 (B) or Tier 3 (D). Although differentiating assessment is as important as differentiating instruction for many students, and it is important to differentiate based on assessment results, universally screening all students and differentiating instruction for all students in Tier 1 are equally important WWC recommendations for RTI, making choice C incorrect.

82. A: Small-group differentiated reading instruction allows students to interact with their peers while also having access to ongoing direct contact with their teacher. When literacy teaching and learning are accomplished through individual interaction (B), this reflects one-to-one reading instruction or intensive individualized intervention. When literacy knowledge is accumulated through contributions from multiple voices (C), this reflects whole-class or large-group instruction. While students may read independently and conduct independent study projects, they should still have some related interaction with their teacher (D).

83. D: When teaching sight words to students with moderate and severe intellectual disabilities, it has been found that community-based instruction helps promote generalization of skills. Generalization is when a student learns a skill in one context and begins to apply it to new contexts,

Copyright © Mometrix Media. You have been licensed one copy of this document for personal use only. Any other reproduction or redistribution is strictly prohibited. All rights reserved.
This content is provided for test preparation purposes only and does not imply an endorsement by Mometrix of any particular political, scientific, or religious point of view.

incorporating it more generally into their thought processes. Students with intellectual disabilities may struggle more to apply skills to broader situations. For instance, they may be successful in learning sight words in the classroom, but they may leave that skill in the classroom instead of applying it out in the community. To help support the generalization process, this student's community should help reinforce that instruction out in the community to demonstrate that the skill can be used in all of life. Choices A and C are incorrect because they are not found to be as effective for students with disabilities as augmented practices, such as community-based instruction. Choice B is incorrect, as orthography refers to the actual writing of letters and less to do with reading skills, and especially sight words. Some teaching strategies may pair reading and writing skills together, but this is even less common for sight word instruction.

84. C: Experts advise that to differentiate reading instruction, teachers should not just reserve read-aloud materials for fun, but use them as common teaching texts (A) for building background knowledge, demonstrating strategy application, introducing issues, and inviting students to journal responses to issues, enabling all students to access needed reading skills and information. They should teach units using multiple texts to meet diverse reading levels (B); reserve 15-30 minutes at least three times a week for independent practice reading at student comfort levels (C); and organize units around topics, issues, or genres instead of basing them on the text (D).

85. C: Skills-focused lessons are effective when they maintain a faster pace (A), are interactive rather than teacher-centered (B), and target the reading skills most critical for each individual reading group (C). While small groups are most common in this lesson structure, teachers use one-on-one instruction, student pairs, and other grouping methods as well (D).

86. D: For reading instruction, flexible small groups can be created by student skill levels within a classroom or across classrooms. Grouping within the classroom is heterogeneous (A); grouping across all classrooms at one grade level is more homogeneous (B). For within-classroom groups, schools can bring in additional materials, staff, and other resources (C) during reading block times for small-group instruction. For across-classroom groups, depending on student needs, students' original classroom teacher or another teacher may give them reading instruction (D).

87. D: Studies have found some CAI not only increases literacy skills, but also attention and interaction in students with disabilities that include autism, cerebral palsy, Down syndrome, and intellectual disability (A). Using multimedia software (e.g., Delta Messages) plus instructional scaffolding is found effective for students not performing well with conventional instruction (B). Combining CAI with the Nonverbal Reading Approach for students with co-existing severe speech disorders and physical disabilities or autism was found effective, but not necessarily more effective than teacher-only instruction or teacher-plus-CAI (C). Acquisition rates depended on individual students, showing the importance of individualizing instruction (D) for this population.

88. A: According to researchers (cf. Cooper 1999, Diamond-CORE 2006), the challenges of changing teacher beliefs regarding reading instruction and initiating a new, research-based reading program arise during the first year of implementation (A). The challenges of refining that new approach, and ensuring that teachers and other staff adhere to program design and implement it consistently, arise in the second year (C). The challenge of addressing teacher "domestication" of a new reading program arises during the third year (A). These experts do not address implementation's fourth year (D); the first three are more challenging.

89. D: The NEA recommends that to promote research-based strategies for developing family-school-community partnerships at the national level, school reform initiatives should put these partnerships at their centers; that not only policy forums, conferences, and comments on federal

Copyright © Mometrix Media. You have been licensed one copy of this document for personal use only. Any other reproduction or redistribution is strictly prohibited. All rights reserved.
This content is provided for test preparation purposes only and does not imply an endorsement by Mometrix of any particular political, scientific, or religious point of view.

regulations, but also policy and legislative proposals, should provide for such partnerships (A); that advocacy for these partnerships in federal legislation is appropriate (B); and that NEA members should disseminate its recommended partnership strategies throughout the Association's membership (C).

90. B: Tier II provides targeted small-group interventions for students who are not meeting grade-level benchmarks, making it the correct answer for students who meet twice a week for focused fluency instruction with a reading specialist. Response to intervention (RTI) is a three-tiered support model that provides increasingly intensive interventions for students who are struggling academically. Tier I includes universal classroom instruction provided to all students. Tier III provides more intensive, individualized support for students who do not respond adequately to Tier II interventions. An individualized education program (IEP) is a special education plan for students who meet eligibility criteria and is not a tier within the RTI model.

Copyright © Mometrix Media. You have been licensed one copy of this document for personal use only. Any other reproduction or redistribution is strictly prohibited. All rights reserved.
This content is provided for test preparation purposes only and does not imply an endorsement by Mometrix of any particular political, scientific, or religious point of view.